Hospitality to Strangers:
Theology and Homosexuality

By

Thomas Kevin Higgs

Table of Contents

INTRODUCTION

In the summer of 2003 the Episcopal Church, in General Convention, shocked the Anglican Communion and the Christian Church around the world by openly affirming the presence, call, baptism, and ministry of gay and lesbian persons in the life of the church by voting in overwhelming support of the Diocese of New Hampshire and their election of the Right Reverend Gene Robinson as their next Bishop. Bishop Robinson is the first Episcopal Bishop elected as an "out" gay man living in a homosexual relationship. Thanks be to God, who is doing a new thing among us in liberation through the power of the Holy Spirit. This movement of the Spirit is a movement for which I have witnessed and prayed diligently for many years. I believe that homosexual people, and their relationships, should be honored as a precious part of God's good creation, and a precious part of the Body of Christ and its ministry. In this book I will defend the full presence, call, baptism, ministry, and integrity of gay and lesbian persons in the life of the church using the Anglican/Wesleyan theological method of an appeal to Scripture, tradition, reason, and experience.

In my journey of academic study and pastoral ministry, I have been blessed with numerous opportunities to engage the church in its relationship with gay and lesbian people. In my study in college and seminary, I have made important, lasting friendships with homosexual people who have completely transformed the negative stereotypes that were engrained in my middle-class Methodist upbringing. In my many years of pastoral ministry, I have been enriched and spiritually nourished in my relationships with many organizations within the ecumenical church community that struggle for full inclusion of homosexual people, such the Reconciling Network and Affirmation in the United Methodist Church and Integrity within the Episcopal Church. Certainly, the most significant opportunity I have had to learn about gay and lesbian people in the context of the church came in my experience as a member of the United Methodist Committee to Study Homosexuality during the 1988-1992

Quadrennium. I and 27 other people from across the church were elected from the General Council on Ministries of the United Methodist Church to study homosexuality. For four years our committee was in dialogue with the great diversity of people of The United Methodist Church, and with persons at the top of their fields in theology, ethics, biblical studies, biology, psychology, and sociology from around the world. We drafted a document that was presented to the General Conference of the United Methodist Church in 1992.[1] Our study committee voted by an overwhelming margin to welcome gay and lesbian persons fully into the life of the church, and reject the current position of the United Methodist Church, which is expressed in *The Book of Discipline* and *Social Principles* with the phrase "Homosexuality is incompatible with Christian teaching."[2] Unfortunately, our study report was not affirmed with the support of the United Methodist Church General Conference. The minority report of our committee was affirmed as the position of General Conference, maintaining the current language in *The Book of Disciple* of the United Methodist Church that rejects full participation of gay and lesbian people in the life of the church. However, the integrity and validity of our study and its original recommendation remains.

As I explore the reality of how the church is in relation to homosexual persons, I do so with a rigorous commitment to the truth as we in the church can understand it. We must look clearly at what can be determined as established evidence and consensus in interpretation within relevant disciplines. The church must not just rest upon what has been handed down to us from the past, but ever explore and question, with critical awareness, the realities of our present understanding as we interpret the Christian faith. To rethink and re-examine the faith constantly is an essential and necessary quality in the life of a faithful disciple and faithful church. Dr. Earl Gossett, my Professor of Theology at Birmingham-Southern College, described this constant re-examination in the life of the church as the heart of the Protestant faith. He described this as making the faith relevant to the present generation. I believe the Church Universal must be open to the movement of the Holy Spirit as we seek God's will and God's Reign in redemption, salvation, and liberation. The Holy Spirit is constantly moving and changing the church.

A simple review of church history demonstrates how and why the church must be open to the Holy Spirit for change: Five hundred years ago the Christian faith, in overwhelming majority, supported the institution of slavery throughout the world. Yet, through critical reflection and a sacrificial witness upon the meaning of our faith in Jesus Christ, today slavery is universally rejected by the Christian Church as oppression and sin. Clearly, the Christian faith changed because of the movement of the Holy Spirit.

The same can be said of the struggle now in place for the position and authority of women in church and society. The Holy Spirit has moved and is moving us still. One hundred and fifty years ago, women were universally subjugated and dominated by a patriarchal church that refused to affirm the full meaning and place of their baptism and ministry within the church. Today, even still, most women throughout the Church Universal cannot serve God as they are called within the Christian church. Thanks be to God that within the Anglican Tradition, the Episcopal Church and the United Methodist Church affirm the position, place, and authority of women as equals with men in the task and blessing of ministry within the church. This liberation for women, like that which is coming for gay and lesbian persons, is the power of the Holy Spirit at work in the church and in the world.

Theological Method:

I will explore the reality of homosexuality through the lens of what has become the established method of theological inquiry within the Anglican tradition. Richard Hooker defended this great tradition in the 16th century with his understanding of the interpretation of our Christian life through the balance of Scripture, Tradition, and Reason. For Hooker, Scripture was the primary authority within the faith, interpreted through tradition and reason. In the Methodist tradition, Wesley incorporated the method begun by Hooker, adding to it the emphasis of the importance of experience, specifically defined as the experience of the work of the Holy Spirit as we live out our lives. This theological method has been described as Hooker's "Three Legged Stool" and as Wesley's "Quadrilateral." In this book, I will explore the reality of homosexual people through the lens of each of these authorities: Scripture, Tradition, Reason, and Experience. In the use of this theological method, I do not use these four authorities as an attempt to "prove" that each of them supports gay and lesbian inclusion in the church. If this debate within the church were that simple, the argument about this divisive issue would have been over long ago. Instead, my argument is a dialogue within and among these four authorities which will demonstrate the brokenness and complexity of each of these authorities and express the need for careful discernment and a prayerful openness to change within the hardened positions of the institutional church. After my examination and argument presented through each of these authorities, I will offer a theology of hospitality, and an agenda for ministry with and by homosexual people as full members and participants at all levels in the life of the church.

Throughout this book, I will insert stories of homosexual people and their families. These stories are true. I either personally knew these individuals in the context of my ministry or heard these individuals tell these stories as participants in the "Listening Posts" held by The Committee To Study Homosexuality of the United Methodist Church. The names and locations have been changed to protect the identity of the individuals.

CHAPTER 1:

SCRIPTURE

Mr. and Mrs. Jones were active members of First United Methodist Church. They were faithful members for most of their life in this church; they raised their children in the church, training their children to be faithful disciples in the church's children and youth departments. When their son, Jeff, graduated from high school he went off to college in another State. In his sophomore year at college, their son "came out" to his parents that he was gay. It was very traumatic for Mr. and Mrs. Jones to hear from their son that he was gay. They struggled emotionally and spiritually with this new reality. Mr. and Mrs. Jones wondered if they had made mistakes raising their son. They wondered how this "change" could have come over Jeff, because they did not see any "signs" of this when he was in high school. They wondered what sort of group Jeff might be associating with in college that might have influenced him to "become gay." Mr. and Mrs. Jones were full of shame that their son was gay; they struggled painfully that somehow they had raised Jeff to think that being gay was acceptable. They went to their pastor at First United Methodist Church for counseling about their son's admission that he was gay. Their pastor was kind and compassionate; however, the pastor agreed with them that this was a terrible thing that their son had become gay and that Jeff had probably been influenced into this sinful behavior. The pastor urged them to encourage their son to go into counseling with a group that claimed to transform gay men back to being heterosexual. After this counseling session with their pastor, the next time Mr. and Mrs. Jones saw Jeff they asked him questions about his sexuality. Jeff told them that he had known that he was gay all of his life. Unfortunately, while growing up, Jeff could not tell them, nor be open to anyone about being gay because of his fear of what would have happened to him: Jeff saw the violence and abuse that happened to other boys who showed signs of being gay in his high school. So Jeff kept this part of himself hidden as deeply as he could. Then, Jeff told his parents that he was dating a very kind and loving student he had met at college, and if it was okay, he would like to bring him home one weekend to meet them. His parents refused. They told him that he could never bring one of his gay friends home with him. At First United Methodist Church, things began to change for Mr. and Mrs. Jones. They did not know how the information got out to the church. Other members of the church seemed to know about what was happening in Jeff's life. Did Jeff's group of hometown friends find out and tell everyone? Was this information spread by the church staff? The secret had been let out. No one knew how the story had been told to the church; however, everyone seemed to know about Jeff's being gay. Mr. and Mrs. Jones noticed a definite change in how other members of the church treated them. They were suddenly given the "cold shoulder" at church events. Even members of the church staff began to avoid them. Mr. and Mrs. Jones' sense of shame about their son's sexuality was reinforced by the behavior of the people at First United Methodist Church. Over the course of the next year, Mr. and Mrs. Jones began to attend church less and less. They no longer felt "at home" at church. It seemed that when they attended any church function they were reminded in informal ways of their shame of having a gay son. As the years passed, Mr. and Mrs. Jones stopped going to church completely. Their son, Jeff, is now a physician, living with his partner in a faithful relationship that has lasted many years. After much hesitancy, Mr. and Mrs. Jones have relented, and allowed their son to bring home his partner on holidays and other occasions.

With both Hooker and Wesley, Scripture is defined within the Anglican tradition as the primary authority in our faith, but not in a narrow Biblical legalism. Neither Episcopalians nor United Methodists are religious "fundamentalists." We do not use the words "infallible," nor "inerrant," nor even "absolute" to describe the witness that is Scripture. We do not worship the Bible; it is not an idol. We affirm that the Bible is a human book, written by people, who could not help but incorporate within the text the culture and bias of their own time. However, in the words of faith, we profess that the Bible is inspired by the Holy Spirit. We call Scripture "Holy" not because everything that is in the Bible is "true" or "correct" as a scientific fact or historical certainty. Instead, Scripture is "Holy" because of the message of God's redeeming revelation, action, and message of salvation that is within it. Scripture is understood as the primary authority in theological discernment in the Anglican/Methodist tradition, in that Scripture is the prophetic and apostolic witness of the revelation of God in the history of the Hebrew people and in the person of Jesus Christ. Scripture is always read in light of historical, literary, and contextual interpretation through a dialogue that exists within an interpretive framework of tradition, reason, and experience. As is affirmed in *The Book of Discipline* of the United Methodist, Tradition, Reason, and Experience *interpret* the apostolic witness of Scripture. There rarely is such a thing as "The Plain Sense" of Scripture. The Bible is *always* interpreted.

For most traditionalists and conservatives in the church, this discussion on issues of sexuality hinges upon the interpretation of the Bible. If you believe that "just because something is in the Bible, then it is absolutely and unconditionally true," then one could understand how a person might say that a homosexual act is a sin, because the few times the Bible mentions homosexual acts, it does so negatively. However, in the Anglican tradition, we do not interpret the Bible as literalists, at least not on other issues, such as divorce or the role of women in the church. We place the Bible in its historical context. We interpret every passage in light of the Biblical witness as a whole and its interpretive context in the life of the church.

Homoerotic Behavior

When using the word "homosexual" we immediately encounter problems in our interpretation of any ancient text. There are significant reasons why the word "homosexuality" should not be used to describe any relationship referenced in the Bible.

Instead, the word "homoerotic" is the best term to describe the behavior mentioned in the New

Testament in relation to same sex behavior. Why? Homoerotic is a preferable term because the reality and existence of what we would describe in the 21st century as "homosexuality" or a "homosexual relationship" or the concept of "sexual orientation" was not a part of the self-understanding of any people in any ancient culture that has been studied. The word homoerotic describes same-sex erotic experiences and relationships that happened in the cultures of the ancient world.[3] Homoerotic **behavior** is not the same as a **committed homosexual relationship**. In the ancient world of the Old Testament, and in the culture of the 1st century of the Common Era, the concept of a stable, socially acknowledged, mutual, committed relationship of people of the same sex (identified in the culture either negatively or positively) was not present. Certainly, since homosexuality has a biological basis, which is demonstrated by scientific inquires on the matter[4], there were people in the ancient world **oriented** toward same-sex relations. However, there is no record from the ancient world of communities or cultures that institutionalized, documented, or recognized committed, monogamous, life-long relationships of people of the same sex. In fact, for both homosexual and heterosexual people, many scholars who study the cultures of antiquity agree that the general concepts of sexual morality, sexuality, and marriage present in the Bible are significantly different from the 21st century concepts of sexual morality, sexuality, and marriage held within a typical mainline Protestant church. Dr. Mary Ann Tolbert, Professor of New Testament at The Pacific School of Religion, concludes:

> The traditions of marriage actually found in the Bible, the ones the Bible does talk about, bear little or no resemblance to what modern Western people understand marriage to do and be today. Marriage between one man and one woman as envisioned by people today was never the ideal relationship in the Bible. Moreover, marriage is not, as some commentators, politicians, and even religious leaders, have recently contended, an "unchanging tradition of thousands of years." Rather, marriage, like all other

social institutions is quite variable and has gone through many different forms over the course of history and across many cultures. For the ancient Mediterranean world from which the Bible came the primary purpose of marriage was the production of legitimate heirs and the management of the household. Sexual compatibility, mutuality, intimacy, and certainly sexual faithfulness, at least for men, were neither values nor concerns of ancient marriage. In the Old Testament or Hebrew Bible, polygamy, the presence of multiple women in the family, was the most common pattern of marriage. Whether we look at patriarchs like Jacob or religious leaders like Moses or kings like David, we have ample evidence for a common pattern of multiple wives. The most formidable example of this pattern can be found in Solomon, David's son, who had, so the Bible tells us, 700 wives and 300 concubines. While concubines were not the same as wives, who produced legitimate heirs for their husband, concubines were officially connected to the husband usually by family contract and were often treated in much the same way as

wives. In addition to all of these
legitimate wives and concubines,
ancient males both in Israel and
Judah and in later Greco-Roman
times had plentiful access to other
sexual workers including slaves
and prostitutes. As the famous
quotation from Greek writer
Demosthenes makes clear: "This is
what it means to be married: to
have sons one can introduce to the
family and the neighbors, and to
have daughters of one's own to
give to husbands. For we have
courtesans for pleasure, concubines
to attend to our daily bodily needs,
and wives to bear children
legitimately and to be faithful
wards of our homes." This multi-
leveled sexual arrangement hardly
describes the current state of
marriage in America, as I think
most people would agree. [5]

There is also diversity in the New Testament
on matters of sexual relations. When we read the
New Testament, the standard of monogamous
marriage as the expected behavior of heterosexual
persons is the norm; however, in St. Paul's letters, he
forcefully concludes that marriage, and sexual

relationships in general, are not the preferred choice for faithful Christians. St. Paul urges those Christians in his churches to "be like him" as a single person, devoting their lives to Christ and God's Reign. St. Paul concludes in 1 Corinthians, chapter 7, that marriage is for the weak and spiritually immature Christian. Obviously, we can see from the witness of Scripture that the understandings, standards, and expectations of how faithful people were to live out their lives as sexual beings is extremely diverse and divided, in both the ancient world and among ancient Jews and Christians, and bear little resemblance to the expectations and assumptions of domestic heterosexism of middle-class America in the 21st century.

It should be noted: One should not conclude from the above discussion that I am opposed to monogamy and faithfulness in marriage. On the contrary, I believe that a faithful, mutual, monogamous, covenant relationship should be the moral standard for all sexual relationships. I support this assumption based upon the witness and teachings of loving faithfulness expressed by Jesus Christ. Where I differ with many in the church is that I assume this standard and expectation, within church and society, can and should be for homosexual people as well as heterosexual people.

Homoerotic Behavior and The Old Testament

When we begin our examination of homoerotic behavior mentioned in the Old Testament, we are greeted with immediate problems. First, as noted above, in the Hebrew Bible we are confronted with the fact that sexuality and its expression institutionalized within ancient Jewish society is almost totally foreign to the assumptions about sexuality and its appropriate expression held by faithful Christians in the 21st century. In the Torah, the dominant, institutionalized form of sexual relations was the practice of heterosexual polygamy.[6] This assertion is shared by the overwhelming consensus of scholars of the Old Testament. And so, from the start, it is difficult to defend a position condemning homoerotic behavior by arguments made from the point of view of the

Old Testament, when the sexual standards explicitly expressed within the heart of the Old Testament are almost universally rejected by modern Christians.

Regardless, in spite of the shaky ground on which stand all arguments about homoerotic behavior based upon the Old Testament, let us proceed with an examination of the usual texts where it is mentioned or referenced in our current argument within the church about homosexuality. In Genesis 19, we have the story of Sodom and the gang of men who sought to have sex with the visitors who were hiding in Lot's house. As the Genesis story unfolds, God destroys the city of Sodom for its wickedness because of the behavior of the men at Lot's house. Among traditionalists in the church, this story had been interpreted as a Biblical rejection of homosexual gang rape, and as such, is a rejection of homosexual relations.

However, when we step back and view the text from the whole of the Biblical witness, we see that this traditionalist interpretation is not the interpretation that is consistently assumed where this Genesis story is referenced in other places in the

Bible. Two of the references to Sodom in other parts of Scripture (Ezekiel 16:49-50; Matthew 10:14-15) support the interpretation that Sodom's sin had nothing to do with homoerotic acts, but was instead the sin of inhospitality to strangers.[7] This "alternative interpretation" is held by many scholars, who say that the story of Sodom was told to illustrate the evil of violating the ancient laws of hospitality: In a nomadic culture, a stranger's life might depend on the hospitality of a stranger's care. Hospitality laws were sacred in the Hebrew Bible. Thus, God's condemnation of the people of Sodom in the Genesis story is about their xenophobic inhospitality.

Beyond this, there are other, significant problems related to Genesis' story of Sodom. How is it possible, or ethical, to suggest that the Christian church of the 21st century should use Genesis' story of Sodom as a cornerstone of sexual ethics, when the response given by Lot to the gang of men wishing to do harm to his guests is to offer his own virgin daughters up to a wild mob to be gang-raped? This story of Sodom and the hospitality of Lot to strangers is so saturated with patriarchal violence and a patriarchal disregard for women that it should be rejected as having any value whatsoever in any discussion of sexual ethics for the Christian Church of the 21st century. Further, when we critically read the Genesis text, we must note that the "men" who were sheltered by Lot were, according to the text, "angels," or supernatural beings. The mob, who wished "To know them" (NRSV translation), wanted to have sexual relations with these "angels." It is significant to some scholars to note that the gang of men in the Genesis passage wanted to have sex with "angels," not with other men. These scholars note that in the ancient world, to have sexual relations with "angels," supernatural beings, or those who represented them (such as a temple prostitute), was to share and gain the spiritual power and spiritual position of the supernatural being. From this perspective, the goal of the gang of men in Genesis' Sodom story was not to have sex with other men, but was "to know" the angels sexually, to dominate them, and take their spiritual power from them.[8] From this point of view, the Sodom story is not about men having sex with men. The Sodom story is about men wanting sex with angels, and in doing so, showing violent disregard of the hospitality laws of the Hebrew Bible.

Also, the context of the story of Sodom is central to its meaning. This is not a story about faithful relationships. This story is about gang-rape, violence, and lack of hospitality. Thus, it seems to me that it should not be associated in any way with any discussion about the meaning and value of committed, monogamous, faithful, loving relationships between two people of the same sex. Because of these considerations, and the above noted patriarchal violence expressed toward women, I am convinced that the Sodom story has little valuable information for the Christian Church of the 21st century as we debate homosexuality, and the place of gay and lesbian people in the life of the church.

Other Old Testament texts often cited by traditionalists within the current debate on homosexual people is the Holiness Code found in Leviticus 18 and Leviticus 20. In Leviticus 18, the text states: *"If a man lies with a male as with a woman, both of them have committed an abomination.*" (NRSV) Leviticus 20 repeats this condemnation. From these texts, traditionalists argue that homosexual acts violate the "order of creation" and divine will. For them, these laws against homosexual acts are theologically grounded in God's revealed order of creation of male and female compatibility.   Thus, to act against God's revealed order is to violate the holiness of God. For traditionalists, as written and revealed in Scripture, this holiness law of the ancient world remains a Scriptural, ethical demand of purity upon all Christians today.[9]

I completely reject this point of view. First, as will be demonstrated in our discussion of the scientific evidence related to homosexuality, it is clearly known that homosexuality is a normal pattern of behavior found throughout the "created order" among humans and non-humans alike. It is a definable, verifiable reality among all mammals that cannot be demonstrated to be maladaptive or pathological within any species.[10] To argue that homosexuality is contrary to "created order" is like the medieval notion that to be left-handed instead of right-handed is contrary to "created order" and is "of the devil," or the Jim Crow assumption that it is the "created order" that ethnic minorities are somehow less human or have less worth than the majority White population: This argument of the "created order" seems to me to be the bigotry of the majority, rationalized, "verified," and codified using theological language. I would caution everyone to be suspicious whenever they hear any point of view based upon a supposed "order of creation" argument. In my experience, this sort of argument is typically theological language used to set up a hierarchy of value that excludes or dehumanizes one or more groups of people. In this sort of language I am reminded of the rejection of Gentiles and the "unclean" by Jewish religious leaders of Jesus' time; the rejection of African-Americans by White Southerners; and the "ethnic cleansing" that happens all over the world, as one group of people defines another as "unclean" because they are outside their culturally defined "created order." It should be noted that Jesus rejected the use of the purity codes of Leviticus in how he related to the so called "unclean" of his day.[11] As we continue our examination of Scripture as our authority in the Anglican/Wesleyan tradition, we will take a closer look at how Jesus treated those people who were rejected by the "purity" religious factions with his faith.

As we conclude our examination of the purity codes of Leviticus, it should be noted that the use of these "laws" from Leviticus is, in my opinion, used in a disingenuous and inconsistent manner by traditionalists within the current argument. In my opinion, these texts are taken from the Bible out of context, and are not applied in an even, equitable manner alongside other "laws" listed in the Book of Leviticus and elsewhere in the Hebrew Bible.

Let us examine this closer: What sort of issues would we be debating if *all* of these purity codes were applied on a consistent basis? As examples, let us look at few hypothetical situations: Let us say, for the sake of argument, I would like to sell my daughter into slavery, as it suggests in the law clearly stated in Exodus 21:7. In the 21st century, what do you think would be a fair price for her? Or, I know that I am allowed no contact with a woman while she is in her period of menstrual "uncleanliness" as is clearly stated in the law from Lev. 15:19-24. The problem is, how do I tell? Should I try asking women about this? Would not most women take offense? Next, the law from Lev. 25:44, which clearly states that I may buy slaves from the nations that are located around us. Some of my more racist neighbors might claim that this applies to Mexicans but not Canadians. If I follow the letter of the law from Leviticus, how do I know? Or, I have a neighbor who insists on working on the Sabbath. According to the law clearly stated in Exodus 35:2, the man should be put to death. Am I morally obligated to kill him myself? Next, the purity code of Lev. 20:20 states that I may not approach the altar of God if I have a defect in my sight. I have to admit that I wear reading glasses. Does my vision have to be 20/20, or is there some "wiggle room" in the law here? And, finally, a friend of mine feels that even though eating shellfish, such as shrimp and lobster, is an abomination according to the law clearly stated in Lev. 10:10 is this a lesser abomination than homosexuality?

As you can see, an even-handed, equitable application of the purity codes of Leviticus is, in truth, rarely attempted. In my opinion, these "laws" are picked out of context, exaggerated by traditionalists in a way never applied in their original use, and emphasized by many religious leaders of today to support their own cultural and personal bias against homosexual people.

If we reject the often-cited texts about homoerotic behavior listed above from the Hebrew Bible as not relevant to the ethical considerations of contemporary relationships of gay and lesbian Christians, what texts from the Old Testament remain important for this discussion? Certainly, the story of liberation from bondage of the Exodus story has great meaning for gay and lesbian people. Also, the dynamics and principles related to covenant and being parts of a covenant community are important for the gay community. However, for me there are two specific areas of prophetic proclamation in the Hebrew Bible that powerfully speak to what it means for the church to have an inclusive attitude toward gay and lesbian people today, leading to the eventual status as full participants in all aspects of the life of the church. These are the virtue and promise of hospitality; and the prophetic call for justice for those marginalized in society.

Hospitality

The virtue of hospitality ranks as one of the highest priorities in the Hebrew Bible. Hospitality is included among "those things of which a man enjoys the fruit of in the world while the principal remains with him in the world to come."[12] The texts from the Hebrew Bible that lift up the importance of hospitality are many: Abraham's welcoming of the three travelers in Genesis 18:1-8 typify the virtue of hospitality in Jewish lore. The Old Testament offers many instances of hospitality to strangers, such as in Judges 13, where Manoah and his wife welcome a man as an angel from God; and 2 Kings 4, where Elisha is shown hospitality by a Shunammite family, and because of this hospitality, Elisha raises their son from death. Within all of these stories from the

Hebrew Bible is the underlying ethical assumption that Israelites are required to show hospitality to those in a strange land because the Israelites were strangers in a strange land. According to Zwi R. J. Werblowsky, the laws of hospitality and the duties of both host and guest are elaborated in both the Hebrew Bible and rabbinic literature: "Hospitality is to be extended to everyone, including the poor, the ignorant, the stranger, and those of lower social status than the host: 'Let your house be open wide, and let the poor frequent it.'" [13] According to the *Shabbat*[14], the phrase now incorporated into the Pesa Seder – "Let all who hunger enter and eat" – was originally the invitation of hospitality to all people uttered before all meals.

With the current stigma placed upon gay and lesbian people in our society, we should consider the reality that homosexual people are "strangers in our midst" in that they are socially, institutionally, religiously, culturally shunned, misunderstood, and discriminated against. Should not the unwavering virtue of hospitality in the Hebrew Bible be a witness to us that God seeks for the church to recognize and listen to the members of our own family who are gay and lesbian, whom we have silenced and/or excluded? It seems to me that the demand for hospitality within the Old Testament should urge the church to open its ears and listen to the people whom we have kept (or pushed) outside the door. If we welcome, listen, and learn, we will discover, to our great surprise, that we have excluded many of our very best, most talented, gifted, spiritually mature family and church members.

Prophetic Justice

Next, the prophetic call for justice for the oppressed is a consistent, dominant theme throughout the Old Testament. Biblical justice is about impartial arbitration, equitable treatment, and a devotion to what is right. Deuteronomy 24:17 instructs the Biblical community never to deprive the stranger or orphan of justice. This demand for justice is perpetual and non-negotiable. Deuteronomy 16:19 identifies the hindrances to justice as favoritism, taking bribes, and ruling in favor of the powerful and privileged against the stranger and the poor. These passages from Deuteronomy demand that the orphan, the stranger, the poor, and subgroups of persons who exist on the margins of society receive unbiased fair treatment by all people. [15]

In the literature of the Psalms, and the Major and Minor Prophets, justice is a socio-ethical norm that is used to critique the interaction among different social groups encountered by and within the Biblical community. The topics of social morality and social economics were major issues. A deep concern is expressed for God's desire for justice for socially weak persons and ostracized groups. Justice in the Prophetic Literature presuppose that oppression, or the perennial disadvantaging of a specific social group, is a major sin. These texts often cite the widow, the stranger, and the orphan as oppressed and marginalized and assert that God is on their side. The prophetic definition of oppression and its circumstances among marginalized people in the Hebrew Bible demand a stop to any activity that dehumanizes or systemically relegates any human being to a position of inferiority.[16] We hear in the prophetic witness of the Old Testament that **all people** should have guaranteed to them equal treatment, an unbiased hearing, and that those on the margins of society, including the "stranger," must be treated fairly with the fullness of dignity and respect.

Clearly, the church does not meet this standard when applied to gay and lesbian people. Homosexuals, even though they are members of our own family, and active in our churches, are "strangers" in our midst, in that we do not know who they are; we typically exclude them as soon as we discover they are present, and we deny them any access to justice in their relationships among themselves and with the rest of society.

Further, the terrible acts of violence and abuse experienced by gay and lesbian persons are a horrific reminder of how homosexual persons are often treated by many in our society. The stories in the media of Matthew Shepherd and Billy Jack Gaither, along with the hundreds of other Hate Crimes documented each year towards gay and lesbian people, should bear down heavily upon the conscience of the church, because we in our rejection and language of inhospitality (such as "incompatible with Christian teaching" in the United Methodist Church) toward gay and lesbian people contribute to and influence further injustice they must suffer. In addition to the rejection of the church, the legal barriers for couples to own property jointly, and even participate in their spouse's funeral arrangement are two of the many painful examples of how homosexual people are denied justice in church and society. It seems to me that the Biblical witness from the Old Testament is that the church should demand simple justice as fairness for gay and lesbian people. In unison with the prophets of the Old Testament, this should be the church's prophetic call.

Homoerotic Behavior and The New Testament

The first point that must be made about the views of the New Testament writers on homoerotic behavior is that this topic is almost never found in the New Testament. Jesus says nothing at all about homoerotic behavior in the Gospels. Also, we find no major discussion of homoerotic behavior in the remainder of the New Testament. There are only three possible references to homoerotic behavior in the New Testament, two from Saint Paul and one in a Deutero-Pauline Epistle; these are Romans 1:26-27, 1 Cor 6:9 and 1 Tim 1:10.

In 1 Corinthians and 1Timothy, supposed references to homoerotic behavior are part of "vice lists" that have serious problems because they rely on an interpretation of a Greek work, *arsenokoites,* whose actual meaning is unknown.[17] There is no other use of this word in existence from any other source in the ancient world. As far as scholars have been able to determine, Saint Paul's use of *arsenokoites* in 1 Corinthians is its first usage in all of Greek literature. Most of the occurrences of the word *arsenokoites* after Saint Paul, from literature of a later time period, are simply a reference to Saint Paul's usage of it in the New Testament.[18]

Some scholars associate the word *arsenokoites* with homoerotic behavior by assuming that it is derived from the Septuagint translation of

Leviticus 20:13, which contains both *arsenos* (male) and *koiten* (bed) in the same sentence. More recent exploration of the word *arsenokoites* by modern scholars has raised considerable question about this understanding of the term, pointing out that to assume the meaning of any word can be made from dividing it up into individual parts is an indefensible textual, linguistic assumption:

> As the debate of homosexuality and Bible has become more explicit, various attempts have been made to defend the interpretation of *arsenokoites* as a reference to male-male or homosexual sex in general. A common error made in such attempts is to point to its two parts, *arsen* and *koites*, and say that "obviously" the word refers to men who have sex with men. Scholars sometimes support this in Greek translations of the Hebrew Bible and in Philo in a context in which he condemns male homosexual sex. Either Paul, it is suggested, or someone before him simply combined the two words together to form a new term for men who have sex with men. This approach is linguistically invalid. It is highly

precarious to try to ascertain the meaning of a word by taking it apart, getting the meanings of its component parts, then assuming, with no supporting evidence, that the meaning of the longer word is a simple combination of its component parts. To "understand" does not mean to "stand under." In fact, nothing about the basic meanings of either "stand" or "under" has any direct bearing on the meaning of "understand." [19]

For us to understand the meaning of *arsenokoites*, the key is not found in recklessly dividing up the word into separate parts, but is instead found in looking closely at how the word is used in its context of Scripture within these "vice lists" found in 1 Corinthians and 1 Timothy. Many scholars support the assumption that the "vice lists" in the Epistles are not random lists; they are instead an ordering of groups of sins or "vices" in which sins of a similar or related nature are listed together.[20] For example, sexual sins are listed together, and economic sins are listed together.

Thus, if the word *arsenokoites* means simply homoerotic sex acts, why does it appear grouped within the list next to economic sins such as theft, robbery and stealing? Thus, if we study the word in the contexts in which this word appears, we can faithfully assume that *arsenokoites* must have had a more specific meaning in Greco-Roman culture than just homoerotic activity in general.[21]

While it is reasonable to conclude that no certainty can be found for the use of the word *arsenokoite* in the New Testament, let us assume for the moment that it might have referred to some kind of economic exploitation by means of sex, perhaps related to some kind of homoerotic activity. One possibility would be that the word refers to male prostitution, especially when the word *arsenokoites* is found next to the Greek word *pornoi* (which has been consistently interpreted to mean prostitution) in the "vice lists" of Saint Paul. [22] However, there is no reference within ancient literature that could confirm this assumption. And, even if this ancient term means male prostitution, the ethical implications and considerations of male prostitution are completely removed from any discussion of the 21st century reality of a committed same-sex relationship between two people who deeply care for each other in a covenant relationship.

Another possibility for the meaning of the word *arsenokoites* is given by Dr. Robin Scoggs, Professor of New Testament at Union Theological Seminary. Dr. Scoggs proposes that the word *arsenokoites* actually refers to the practice of pederasty, which was a common practice in the Greco-Roman world of older men using teenage boys as sexual partners. There is a significant body of literature that demonstrates the frequency of this practice in Greek culture, even though there is no reference to this practice using the word *arsenokoites*.[23] The act of pederasty is an act of dominance and submission in the context of an abusive relationship between an adult and a minor. Again, this abusive practice in the ancient world is simply not comparable to the 21st century reality of a loving, mutual, committed, monogamous covenant relationship between two adults of the same sex.

Thus, because of our inability to find any supportive or conclusive evidence to confirm any assumption about what the word *arsenokoites* actually means in the context of its brief usage in the Epistles, this word must be set aside as having any helpful assistance for us in the discussion of homoerotic behavior within the New Testament.

Because of this, the only New Testament passage that has any useful information regarding the church's rejection of homosexual relationships is the brief passage in Romans, where Saint Paul discusses sexual behavior in Chapter 1: 26-27. In verse 26, Saint Paul speaks of "their women exchanging natural intercourse for that which is against nature." If Saint Paul is speaking here of female homoerotic behavior, then it is the only verse in the entire Bible even to mention that subject. However, there is great controversy and uncertainty in this text as well. Most of the early writings of the church who discussed this text, and some modern scholars as well, assume that Saint Paul was speaking about what we today would call heterosexual relations, in which these women were exchanging normal sexual intercourse with men, which could lead to pregnancy, for sexual relations which could not, such as anal or oral sex.[24] However, among scholars there is great diversity of opinion here: Several modern scholars, citing the parallel with verse 27, which explicitly says that men were exchanging natural relations with women for lust for other men, argue that Saint Paul was indeed referring here to female homoeroticism, even if later Church Fathers did not always read him that way. [25]

As we read the many points of view about the Romans 1:26-27 passage, it seems fair to conclude that this passage is a rejection of some sort of homoerotic behavior by Saint Paul. However, the arguments related to it are varied and widely speculative, and the context of this homoerotic behavior referenced in the text is unknown, although most scholars assume it describes some sort of casual, promiscuous sexual behavior. It must be pointed out, even with this verse, that what Saint Paul might have considered "natural" sexual relations are very different from our understandings of "natural" sexual relations in the 21st century.

Saint Paul's reference to the fact that these people "exchanged" natural relations for those "against nature," demonstrates his close connection with the understanding of sexuality prevalent in the ancient world. In the ancient Greco/Roman world, sexual "orientation" was an unknown concept. In the Greco/Roman world, proper sexual relations were determined primarily by social standing or status rather than by gender or "orientation." Sexuality was always understood to be the combination of dominance and submission; consequently, "natural" sexual relations occurred only between socially dominant persons and socially submissive persons. [26] Since women were assumed in that culture to be "by nature" submissive, the sexual relation of a free man with a woman was always "natural," as were sexual relations between free men and slaves (either male or female) and, at least in classical Greece, between free men and boys. The central moral issue of sexuality from the ancient world, both Roman and Jewish, was any attempt to reverse those "natural" roles. For a man to have sex with another adult man meant one of them would have to be penetrated like a woman, a shameful and degrading position in the culture of the ancient world. For women to have sexual relations with other women meant someone would have to be the "man" or "penetrator," a pretentious act of pride and shamelessness in the culture of the ancient world. As one born and educated in the ancient world, Saint Paul believed that all people were capable of natural sexual relations, in which the "natural" roles of the dominant person and the submissive person were honored, but that some people willfully gave up those natural roles to take the dishonorable position, which was against their "nature." In reflecting on this ancient argument against homoerotic behavior, which seems to lie behind Saint Paul's own views, it is important for us in the present 21st century world to notice the extent to which this argument rests on an overwhelmingly oppressive foundation of sexism, because the submissive, penetrated role of women was so despised, any man who willingly took that position had to be deeply perverted.[27] I fear that sexism, and the suspicion placed upon people who do not fulfill traditional gender roles, still lies behind much of the hostility and bigotry directed toward gay men and lesbians in the church and society today.

The focus of the first chapters of Romans is to teach us, Gentile and Jew, that we are all sinners who stand in need of the saving grace of God in Jesus Christ. Thus, it seems to be an odd misuse of Saint Paul to read this passage as singling out homosexual people as sinners, while all others are somehow righteous in God's sight.

However, even if we assume that there is at least one clear reference in the New Testament to the "sinful" nature of homoerotic desire, does this one passage justify the formation of a church policy excluding such people from the full fellowship of the church? It seems clear that this passage from Romans refers to acts of promiscuity of sexual relations outside the boundaries of covenant faithfulness of any kind. Is it fair to condemn all gay and lesbian relationships in the 21st century by using this text? What about the millions of gay and lesbian people who live in faithful, monogamous, committed relationships, who share a deep relationship of life-long love?

It seems to me to be an oppressively unjust practice to use this one passage from Romans to label and generalize all gay and lesbian relationships as sinful, because this one passage from the Bible is not representative in any way of the integrity and faithfulness demonstrated in gay and lesbian relationships. The "abuse" of this passage is how it is used in ways never intended. It is used out of context, in ways that are destructive to the larger church and its Gospel witness. To use this passage to condemn the relationships of gay and lesbian people would be very much the same as taking the Bible passage from 1st Corinthians, where women are ordered to be silent (1 Corinthians 14:34) out of context, and then creating a mandate for the whole church where all women would be required to be silent at all times. Again, the use of this one passage from Romans to reject all gay and lesbian persons from full participation in the church is very much like the usage of Scripture by 19th century slave-owner churches of the American South, taking the few passages in the Epistles that affirm the institution of slavery (Eph. 6:5; Col. 3:22; Tit. 2:9; 1 Pet.2:18) as a justification of their own horrific practice. Such usage, then and now, is about taking Scripture out of its 1st century context, and using the Bible as a tool of oppression.

Homoerotic Behavior vs. Re-Marriage

To bring forward the issue of justice, Dr. Mary Ann Tolbert, Professor of New Testament at Pacific School of Religion, in her defense of gay and lesbian persons within the context of the United Methodist Church, offers a short comparison with another controversial issue in the New Testament which might be helpful: Divorce and remarriage.[28] Professor Tolbert observes the general and long-standing practice in all "main-line" Protestant churches of affirming the divorce and the re-marriage of divorced persons in the church. However, she points out that if we look at the New Testament witness on this issue we find abundant confirmation of its sinfulness. In each of the synoptic Gospels, Jesus forbids divorce and asserts that anyone who marries a divorced person commits adultery (Matthew 5:31-32; 19:3-9; Mark 10:11-12; Luke 16:18), a violation of one of the Ten Commandments. In the Gospel of Matthew, Jesus twice issues this prohibition, once in the Sermon on the Mount (Matthew 5:31-32) and again in a controversy with lawyers who argue that Moses allowed such measures (Deuteronomy. 24:1-4). While in Matthew, Jesus seems to alter his decree by allowing a special exemption for "unchastity" (Gk: *porneia*), in Mark and in Luke the decree is categorical: No divorce is allowed and anyone who marries a divorced person commits adultery, a sin about which the entire Bible has much to say. Saint Paul knows of this command and repeats it in its categorical form for the Corinthians (1 Corinthians 7:10-11). Except for wondering what Matthew might have intended by "unchastity," there is no scholarly debate over the meaning of the words used in these passages nor the clear demands of the passages themselves. Thus, the New Testament authority of

Jesus and Saint Paul both are adamantly clear that divorce is forbidden to followers of Jesus and additionally that the remarriage of a divorced person constitutes adultery, a serious sin. Yet, in Protestant churches all over this country, Protestant clergy are conferring the church's blessings on unions which the New Testament clearly calls adulterous.

Professor Tolbert compares these two issues. On the one hand, we have one clear verse in Saint Paul's letter to the Romans that condemns homoeroticism as sinful, which constitutes the entire reliable witness of the New Testament on the topic. Based at least in part on such Biblical authority, most Protestant churches have decided to prohibit its clergy from blessing unions of gay men or lesbians. On the other hand, we have clear sayings and stories in each of the synoptic Gospels and in Saint Paul's letters which categorically forbid divorce and remarriage for followers of Jesus, and yet, few "Main-Line" Protestant churches or clergy are prohibited from celebrating and blessing such unions; indeed, according to Biblical authority, most Protestant churches and clergy daily place their blessing on these "adulterous" relationships. For Professor Tolbert, the radically, even wildly, different treatment these two issues, and the people affected by them, receive under present rulings of most churches would have to be evaluated by any fair person as profoundly unjust. It seems to both Professor Tolbert and me that the deep inconsistency of the use of the Bible in present church policy has indeed created a situation of clear injustice and hypocrisy.

The Inclusive Witness of the New Testament

Over and again in the heated argument within the church about the place of lesbians and gay men, there is a constant barrage of reference from traditionalists within the church to the "negative" or supposedly critical texts of Scripture found in the few Biblical texts that reference behavior related to homosexual acts. However, what is most often overlooked in this argument is the larger body of scriptural reference to the inclusive witness found in the ministry of Jesus, and the hospitality shown to *all* people in the life of the early church, especially those people marginalized by religious elites. Over and again in the struggles of Jesus, and in the conflicts and struggles in the life of the early church, we see the movement of the Spirit to overcome barriers of exclusion.

If we were to scan the witness of the actions of Jesus portrayed in the Gospels, we can say with absolute certainty that Jesus not only associated with, but was primarily in ministry with and for the marginalized, humiliated people, those labeled, shunned, and excluded by the religious authorities as "sinners." Jesus welcomed the excluded stranger and the outcast as beloved in his own community. The Gospels agree on the fact that Jesus associated with and regularly had table fellowship with a general group described as "tax collectors and sinners" or sometimes just "sinners" (see, e.g., Matthew 9:10-11; 11:19; Mark 2:15-17; Luke 5:30; 7:34; 15:1; 18:13-14). John Dominic Crossan describes this behavior as "open commensality" where everyone, at every social strata, was welcome in the community begun by Jesus to share table fellowship and hospitality as a radical challenge to the existing social/cultural religious status-quo. [29]

The New Testament Gospels portray a group of powerful Jewish leaders in authority over the beliefs of the people, including Pharisees, scribes, Sadducees, and Temple Chief Priests. According to the Gospels, this group rejected other Jews whom they defined as "sinners" and refused to have any contact with them because their actions violated the Law of Moses, especially the "purity codes" which defined some people as "unclean." The category of "sinners" included people we might today think of as "sinners," such as adulterers, thieves, and murderers. However, the largest portion of the group were probably people whose occupations or living situations prevented them from keeping the Law, like tax-collectors, who were assumed to steal from their tax collection and had close dealings with Gentiles, who were also considered "unclean." The list of "sinners" continued with lepers, people who had any physical deformity, and people of low status and/or low economic means who could not maintain the "cleanliness" standards demanded by the Law (similar to our homeless/destitute street-people in 21st century America?). We see in the behavior of the religious authorities the violence embedded in the religious institutions of Jesus' day. This institutionalized violence is manifested in the rejection of the poor as outcasts of society, unwelcome in places of worship, and stigmatized by the theological concepts and ecclesiological behavior embraced by the religious culture of that time.

By eating with these people, Jesus was not only showing hospitality, Jesus was acting radically and prophetically. To share table fellowship in ancient Jewish culture was a declaration of friendship and equal status. Thus, in eating with "sinners" Jesus was declaring himself one of them and declaring them his equals in status.[30] It is important to recognize that Jesus did not demand they change occupations or social status in order to have this fellowship with him: tax-collectors remained tax-collectors, Gentiles remained Gentiles; the "unclean" remained "unclean," and, the destitute remained destitute.[31] Indeed, it is precisely Jesus' radical inclusion of those whom the majority of

Jewish authorities rejected as unclean or unworthy that, according to the Gospels, deeply angered the Jewish authorities and led to their rejection of him.

As the New Testament Gospels present the story, it would be fair to say that Jesus' acts of disobedience to those with religious authority, by his radical inclusion of those marginalized and rejected by that tradition, was one element that led directly to his crucifixion. To demonstrate God's equal love for those whom traditional religious authorities rejected as unclean sinners, Jesus was willing to risk his life, and die on the cross.

To see how Jesus treated the outcasts of his society, and took great risks to include them within his fellowship, is an illustration for us today how Christians should treat homosexual people. Lesbians and gay men are currently marginalized, prevented from ordination, and seen by many as "unclean" sinners. The official authority of most Protestant churches has formalized their marginalization and humiliation by preventing its clergy from blessing their unions of love and life-long fidelity. To offer this group not just simple hospitality but radical inclusion in the full life of the Christian community just as they are, without demanding that they become who they are not, would seem similar to Jesus' prophetic acts of table fellowship with "sinners" in the New Testament.[32] To take such prophetic action, Jesus was willing to risk his life. Yet, almost two thousand years after Jesus' crucifixion, the church founded by him continues to marginalize gay and lesbian people, and refuses to follow his prophetic example of radical hospitality by fully welcoming and affirming *all* people and their faithful relationships.

In responding to the Biblical witness, we are never apart from the delicate task of interpretation and discernment. From the many voices that we hear, it is important for us to define clearly which voice has priority. John Wesley taught that in the interpretation of Scripture, the Old Testament should be interpreted by the New Testament, and the New Testament should be interpreted by the Gospels. It is Jesus' voice that should have the highest priority in the ethical, theological debates of the church. When we follow this method on the issue of homosexuality, then we are guided by the radical hospitality of Jesus. For me, the word of Biblical truth is how Jesus embraced the abused and the outcast, the ones the religious authorities said were "unclean," and welcomed them with complete hospitality. Jesus loved them in the fullness of God's grace, told them they were children of God, and called them to faithful discipleship: To love God with all their heart, mind, and soul; and to love their neighbor as they love their self.

An Examination of Mark 11:15-19

The "Cleansing of the Temple" is one of the most significant acts in the ministry of Jesus. It is attested to by every Gospel. The Gospel of St. Mark describes this event as Jesus' first act during the week we call Holy Week. In the Gospel of St. Matthew and St. Luke the "Cleansing of the Temple" happens on Palm Sunday, immediately after Jesus' entry into Jerusalem. In the Gospel of St. John, this event is so important and symbolic that it is portrayed as one of the first things done by Jesus in his ministry. I believe this confrontation with

Temple practice is probably the one event that sealed Jesus fate in the minds of the religious and political authorities of Jerusalem. After this, the leaders knew they must kill Jesus. He was just too dangerous.

To understand the importance and the meaning of the "Cleansing of the Temple" we must understand what the Temple meant to the Jewish people. The Temple in Jerusalem was the most important structure in the Jewish national identity. Physically, it was the largest group of buildings in the city, dominating the skyline of ancient Jerusalem. As the sun set upon ancient Jerusalem, the last structure to catch the rays of the sun was the Pinnacle of the Temple set upon the Temple Mount. There glowing in the golden light, the polished stone and gold-laid wood would stand alone as the pride of the Jewish people.

Spiritually, the Temple was the center of the Hebrew faith. The Temple was where the priests offered sacrifices to God following the precise instructions of the Torah. The Temple contained the Holy of Holies, where no one could enter except once a year, when the High Priest went in to pray for the forgiveness of the sins of the nation. The Holy of Holies was where many Jews believed God actually resided. Nothing was more important to the Jewish people than the Temple in Jerusalem.

The context of the "Cleansing of the Temple" in the Synoptic Gospels has it as one of the last and most extreme of a series of conflicts between Jesus and the religious and political leaders. That fateful year, probably 30 A.D., Jesus and his disciples came up to Jerusalem for the Passover. According to the Gospels, Jesus was at the height of his popularity. He had come from Galilee preaching the kingdom of God, healing and feeding the people, with a message of God's grace and righteousness.

According to the Gospels, Jesus was welcomed into Jerusalem by his followers as the Messiah. This entrance, of course, made the Romans very suspicious, for this was an act that challenged their occupation of Palestine. In the hearts and minds of the Jewish people, to hail someone as Messiah was a direct act of sedition against Rome. And then, Jesus' first act in the city of

Jerusalem was to start a disturbance in the Temple. To the shock and surprise of Jesus' followers and the religious authorities, Jesus confronts the operation of the Temple. He turned over the tables of the money changers; he chased out those who are overseeing the Temple sacrifices; he accuses the High Priests and scribes of being thieves and robbers.

It is hard for us to put Jesus' radical act into a modern context. Perhaps it was as radical as Martin Luther King, Jr. marching into racist Birmingham, Alabama, during Holy Week in 1963, demanding Civil and Human Rights for African-Americans? Why in the world would Jesus do such a thing? Why create such a scene? If he had a little political savvy about him, could Jesus have rubbed elbows with the religious elite and gained influence? Maybe he could have secured a position for himself; or at least found a few supporters among those with influence, such as the Pharisee Nicodemous, who sought Jesus out during the night. Why start a fight with those in authority? After all, this was the Temple, the spiritual home of Jewish people!

A number of scholars such as Marcus Borg, John Dominic Crossan, Bruce Malina, Ched Myers, and Richard Rohrbaugh give us insights from the history, archeology, and sociology of the 1st century, and help us understand how the Temple worked, and give us an understanding why Jesus did what he did.[33]

Here is how the Temple worked: The people would come to Jerusalem during the Passover festival, and, having saved up their money during the year (which was a considerably difficult task for the poor people of Palestine) they would use this money to pay their Temple dues or tax and also use the money to buy animals such as doves or lambs to be sacrificed at the altar. This was their religious obligation. The Gospels give witness to this requirement: Everyone had to pay the Temple dues. Even the poor widow, dropping in her "widow's mite," had to pay the Temple tax. The Temple dues and sacrifices were an essential part of this religious culture. The Jewish people were taught by their religious tradition that the only way they could be in a right relationship with God, the only way they could find atonement with God, would be to participate in the Temple sacrifice and worship.

To participate in the Temple, these pilgrims were required to go to the money changers in front of the Temple. The money changers, for a fee, changed their money from the Roman coins, which could not be used in the Temple because they had the image of the Roman Emperor on them, into Temple tokens that could be used to pay and purchase sacrifices in the Temple. This "Temple economy" of money changers and buyers and sellers of sacrifices was central to the experience of the Temple under Roman occupation.

However, the witness of history tells us that this "Temple economy" was thoroughly corrupt.[34] The money changers and the Priests took a percentage of the money. These religious elites became rich through the fees charged to the pilgrims when the pilgrims entered and participated in the Temple worship. Jesus accuses them in Mark 12:40 of "devouring the widows' houses" through their practices in the Temple. And here is a central issue for Jesus: Because of the fees and high cost of the sacrifices, the reality became that many people could not participate in Temple worship. Many did not have enough money. The overwhelming majority of the population in Palestine was poor, with a large percentage of them destitute. If you were destitute, you could not buy the proper sacrifice or pay the temple dues. This "Temple economy" became a barrier for the poorest people to enter the Temple. Thus, the very poor of ancient Palestine could not bring themselves, through sacrificial worship, following ancient Jewish tradition, into a right relationship with God.

Compounded upon this barrier to the Temple were the Purity Laws of the Torah, strictly enforced by the Temple. If you were a leper or had any disease or condition that made you "unclean" according to the religious authorities' interpretation of the Law of Moses, you were prohibited from worship in the Temple unless you went through a time consuming, expensive process of purification. The Temple tax and the cost of an animal to be sacrificed was so high, that those who were unclean or poor because of their physical condition could earn enough money to participate in the Temple sacrifice; they could not bring themselves through sacrifice into a right relationship with God. If you were a Gentile, you could not participate in worship in the Temple. Yes, Gentiles could enter into the "Court of the Gentiles" of the Temple; however, they were barred from full participation in the Temple.

Thus, in 1st century Palestine, the result of all of these oppressive barriers of exclusion was that the Temple had become the primary enforcer of a religious hierarchy of purity that defined most people as not redeemed in the sight of God.[35] The Temple had become the institution that justified as acceptable before God barriers of segregation between different people and different groups of people. The Temple, that mighty and beautiful structure, with its pious religious practices, was at that time a barrier between God and the people, rather than an instrument of atonement with God for all the people.

In addition to this, the priests and scribes who operated this Temple economy, being wealthy through these practices, were living a privileged life in a collaborative relationship with the brutal Roman army of occupation, while most every other Jew in Palestine lived in poverty and oppression. Because of this corruption, because of this separation and barrier from the cultic practices that connected the people to God, enforced by the religious authorities, Jesus rejected the practices taking place in the Temple as unacceptable in the sight of God. For Jesus, the Temple no longer did what it was supposed to do. Instead of connecting the people to God, instead of being that place where people could find God, the Temple practices had become a barrier to a relationship with God for many, many people. Jesus would not stand for it. According to the Gospel of Mark, Jesus proclaimed, "this Temple is supposed to be a house of prayer for all nations, and you have turned it into a den of thieves." The message of Jesus in this text is that there will be no barriers between God and the people; there will be no barriers of segregation between groups of people.

This radical act of Jesus in the Temple calls forth within us today a radical re-evaluation of our religious practices and institutions.   In what way do we, in the name of God and by the power of religious institution, set up barriers between God and the people because of our pious notions of purity, guilt and shame, economic barriers, elitism, or sexuality? In what way do we, in the practice of pious religion, separate and define as unworthy our neighbor because they are poor, or different, of another nationality or race, or of a minority sexual orientation? The Gospels show us that Jesus will have none of this sort of "religious" behavior. Jesus' action at the Temple is a loud and public proclamation that the Reign of God is open to all people, unconditionally. It seems to me that an honest reading of this text demands that the House of God (and the church of the 21st century) shall be a house of prayer for all people, a house of equality and hospitality for every nation, every language, every gender, every sexual orientation, every so-called level of status, and especially for the poor, the marginalized, the "unclean," and the outcast.

CHAPTER 2:

TRADITION

William was an Episcopal Priest. He was born into a conservative, wealthy, privileged family, and attended the finest private schools throughout his life, from kindergarten through seminary. William as a child, loved going to church. The beauty and pageantry of the Anglo-Catholic tradition moved and inspired him deeply. Early in his life, William felt a call to the priesthood, and attended college, and then on to seminary with the singular intention of becoming an Episcopal priest. Yet, William had a terrible secret that he had to hide: William was burdened with intense homosexual desires. As early as he could remember thinking about sex, William thought about other men. Of course, William had been very carefully taught by family and church that homosexuality was a sin. William, as a teenager, did much research about the Biblical passages that mentioned homosexual behavior, and was firmly convinced that God considered homosexuality an abomination. William kept this secret of his sexual desires from everyone, and did all he could to portray himself as a respectable Christian man who would never participate in such behavior. While William was in college he unexpectedly became close friends with another student in his classes. Even though William had powerful desires to be physically near this young man, he resisted these desires fiercely. One night while studying together, the other young man made a sexual advance toward William. William had been so obsessed with his own denial and false portrayal of himself, that he was unaware that the young man whom he had been drawn to as a close friend, was also struggling with his homosexual identity. William and the other young man had a sexual encounter that night. This experience overwhelmed William with confusion, pain, and shame. William broke off the friendship with this young man, and never spoke to him again. William recommitted himself to leading a chaste, pure, heterosexual life. William devoted himself to his studies. He attended seminary, graduating with highest honors. William was ordained an Episcopal priest, and began serving as Assistant Priest at the most conservative parish in his diocese. There, William found a faith community committed to opposing the "homosexual agenda" that was gaining strength in the Episcopal Church. William became a powerful spokesperson against homosexuality, and often mentioned this issue in his sermons. William is now married with children. In 2003, when the Episcopal Church ordained the Right Reverend Gene Robinson, an "out" gay man, as Bishop of the Diocese of New Hampshire, William left the Episcopal Church and joined an offshoot "Anglican" church that is committed to the "traditional" stance of the church against homosexuality.

Within this theological framework of the Anglican tradition, whether Hooker's "Three Legged

Stool" or Wesley's "Quadrilateral," tradition is defined as the history of the interpretation of the faith within the church. Tradition as an authority is not merely a ridged allegiance to the orthodox, or "majority" tradition within our history. Rather, we must learn from the witness of all of the tradition of the church. Tradition as authority embraces and learns from the "minority report," the opinions and perspectives that did not "win out" in the theological struggles that have existed throughout history. For example, Tradition as an authority includes both the witness of the Methodist-Episcopal Church of the North and its struggle against slavery; as well as the reality of the Methodist-Episcopal Church South and its endorsement of slavery, oppression, and domination in the name of God. We learn from the tradition of both. We learn from their successes and their failures. We learn from the tradition of the history of our creeds and how they were formed by the leadership of the dominant church. We also learn from the stories of the "underside" of our history, such as the power, presence, and leadership of women in the life of the early church, as well as the centuries of oppression and brutality shown women as they were (and are) rejected from places of authority in the life of the church. We learn that some ideas, though once thought of as acceptable tradition and teaching, are no longer valid.

Dr. Dwight Vogel, Professor of Theology at Garrett-Evangelical Theological Seminary, agrees:

> For me, Tradition refers not to the traditions which churches, or even the church, has, but with the dominant thrust of the church's teaching. The church does not always understand what is central and what is tangential at any given time. There have been periods when the church has thought that the view that the earth revolved around the sun was heresy, or that there was an implicit approval of slavery within the Tradition. We have no qualms about saying the church was wrong in these regards, that it misunderstood the nature of its own Tradition. We are called upon to discern, with the help of the Holy Spirit, what is central to the Tradition of the church and what is culturally conditioned baggage, which we have confused with that Tradition. [36]

To study the tradition of the church is to take a long view that many times shocks us, with its history of brutality and political violence, while at the same time surprises us with the presence of diversity and divergence in how the church has defined issues of sexuality throughout its history. In many ways, to view Tradition as an authority in the church is to often place oneself on one side of history arguing against another opposing point of view.

Christian Ethics

Tradition as authority within our common life as Christians is also an appeal to the discipline of Christian Ethics. There are great traditions in ethics written through the ages that define our moral, ethical responsibilities, and guide our actions. Often the language of ethics can be cumbersome and difficult. Teleological or ontological arguments, or other language and descriptions can be hard for the "layperson" to grasp. However, in some cases, for the "person in the pew," the reality of Christian Ethics and the necessity of moral guidance for our daily life can be simply asked using the popular phrase: "What would Jesus do?" The simple answer is to follow Jesus' commandments: love your neighbor (even if he/she is your enemy), care for the poor, hunger and thirst for what is right, seek first the kingdom of God. In Jesus' teachings and parables we have our basic foundation for Christian ethics.

In the area of sexuality, especially homosexuality, what are we to do? How are we to understand how homosexual people are to relate as faithful Christians to each other sexually? Dr. Joseph Monti, in his book *Arguing About Sex*, reflects upon this question:

> Only by engaging in a full range of moral speech, including clearly disclosed rather than systematically distorted attention to the narrations of homosexual persons, will we find whether the burdens of celibacy now being *imposed* on homosexual Christians by many Christian denominations are morally necessary or not. In

this debate we cannot avoid a
critical examination of the state of
the Church's moral rhetoric of
homosexuality. My argument
throughout has been that the
present discourse of the
denominations discloses significant
confusions. Christian sexual ethics
is no longer as sure as it once was
of the relation between norms and
rules for moral guidance in sexual
matters in general and especially
with respect to the question of
homosexuality.[37]

It seems to me that Jesus' ethical teachings

about how people were to be in relationship were

simple and direct. He taught us to love our neighbor

in the context of intimate/family relationships with a

devotion to faithfulness. Life-long faithfulness is the

demand of Jesus in the context of marriage and

friendship. Although Jesus never spoke a word

about what we call homosexuality or homoerotic

acts, in every relationship Jesus taught or spoke

about, he put an emphasis on loving, covenant

faithfulness in a context of justice and righteousness.

Jesus taught us not only how to be spouses and

friends one to another, but also the importance of loving our enemy. It seems to me that in both our sexual behavior, and in our extended social behavior, the ethic of loving, mutual, covenant faithfulness should be affirmed. For me, the tradition of ethical, moral truth that should guide us is how Jesus embraced the abused and the outcast, the ones the religious authorities said were "unclean." Jesus extended and affirmed covenant faithfulness to them. Jesus loved them, told them they were children of God, and called them to faithful discipleship. This is an ethic of justice, reconciliation, faithfulness, and hospitality. In seems only fair that the same values and ethical demands followed by heterosexual couples should also be extended to sexual ethics for all people, regardless of their sexuality.

Often in the context of the debate on homosexuality in the church, I am attacked by opponents as supposedly abandoning the moral and ethical traditions of sexuality that have marked the faith since its beginning. This is not true. The demand of living a moral, faithful life in the context of covenant faithfulness is the same for *all* people, heterosexual or homosexual. In fact, my argument is that the church must offer a marriage service for gay couples as a necessity to help gay couples maintain their covenant faithfulness in a culture that is often destructive of long-term faithful commitments. All one has to do is look at the divorce rate among married heterosexuals to see how difficult covenant faithfulness is for most persons. Gay couples, just like heterosexual couples, need the blessing and support of the church in order to maintain faithful, moral, and ethical long-term relationships. There are so many people who condemn homosexual persons because of the stereotype of a promiscuous "gay culture" held by mainstream America, while at the same time offering no means by which to help support, solidify, and institutionalize the healthy, monogamous, committed relationships that homosexual persons build.

Tradition: A Theology of Atonement

One of the central affirmations in Christian Tradition is the theology of atonement. I understand the theology of atonement as the church's expression of how God and humanity, and even the whole of creation, are "made one" with each other. The theology of atonement then becomes the way the church speaks about how God has done the work of redeeming creation, making us whole again, restoring creation and humanity so that we might be and become what God created us to be. Atonement is about being in "right relationship" with God and with other people. In almost universal agreement, theologians throughout the length and depth of Christian Tradition agree that the reality of atonement is an act of God, by which God, through God's own work, makes all creation one through the life, death, and resurrection of Jesus Christ. The diversity in Christian Tradition is in the differing understandings of how God does this atonement through Jesus Christ.

One of the essential aspects of any critical understanding of Christian Tradition and Christian theology is that our theological understanding, its images and assumptions all bear consequences and implications in our common life. How we understand the way God works bears consequences for us in the church. How we understand the work of God molds the way we relate to each other in profound ways. How we understand the way God works in Jesus Christ, in the church, and within each person bears with it underlying values and affirmations that impact us all. It is my assumption that these values, affirmations, consequences implicit in each theology should be critically examined and analyzed carefully so that the images, models, and theological systems we affirm effectively "carry the faith" in our common life in the Christian journey. It is also my assumption that just because a specific theological understanding of atonement has been celebrated and affirmed in the past by some Christian Community, does not necessarily mean that it is normative and faithful to the Gospel for all time, or, that it can "carry the faith" into the future. There are different atonement theories and traditions in the life of the church. Which ones best "carry" the faith? Which ones damage and harm the faith?

In this chapter, my focus is upon the meaning of atonement for gay and lesbian persons in the life of the church. What is implied in the atonement theories of the Tradition of the church for gay and lesbian persons? What are the assumptions, values, implications, and consequences for gay and lesbian persons that are different from heterosexual persons? Do the underlying theological assumptions of an atonement theory mold the response of the church in such a way that gay and lesbian persons are damaged or threatened by it? For example, if an atonement theology has as its primary values punishment and violence, does this have specific implications for gay and lesbian people, whose sexuality is defined as intrinsically evil and sinful by the leadership of the church? And if this is the case, should any atonement theory in the Christian church accentuate punishment and violence for any reason?

In their experience of the Christian church, homosexual people have almost universally been denied access to membership, participation, and affirmation as their whole selves (out and open) in the life of the church. Further, because a person's sexual identity and orientation cannot be separated from what it means to be a person, homosexual persons are defined by the theology of the church as unable to come into "right relationship" with God and other people because their sexuality has been labeled as either intrinsically evil, sinful, "dysfunctional," outside of God's acceptable design for sexual relationships, and/or "incompatible with Christian teaching."

Because the rejection of homosexual persons has been codified into church law and implemented in severe discrimination in the life of the church, homosexual persons have been forced to deny themselves and pretend they are someone other than who they are (closeted), or leave the church to make their way outside the church's boundaries and relationships. In either of these scenarios, people who are homosexual have had to separate themselves emotionally and/or physically from the Christian life experienced in the church, or bond together in a "gay church" separate from other Christians. In any event, homosexual persons are denied the redemptive relationship of experiencing their atonement in the life of the larger church:

They are not "At One" with their Christian neighbors, not necessarily because of what they do, but because of who they are at the center of their being, and because of what has been done, and is being done by the church. It seems to me that the behavior of the church towards gay and lesbian people can be described as institutionalized spiritual violence against homosexual people.

How does a theology of atonement contribute to this destructive pattern? Is this pattern of rejection and abuse within the church related to a theology of atonement also found with other marginalized, outcast groups in society? And, if this pattern is found elsewhere, are there similarities? As we proceed, I will define the dominant classical theologies of atonement; discuss the values, affirmations, consequences, and implications found in these theologies; inquire how these impact the homosexual community, and propose a theology of atonement that is both consistent with our Christian heritage and faithful to the ministry of Jesus with the marginalized and outcast.

A History of Theories of Atonement

In classical Christian theology, humanity's reconciliation with God is understood primarily as achieved through the sacrificial death of Jesus Christ. The operative word is *sacrifice*. The teaching of the classical theories of atonement is rooted in the understanding that Jesus was a *sacrifice* for the sake of humanity, so that humanity might be in "right relationship" with God. Although it should be noted that even though all classical atonement theories focus upon the sacrifice of Jesus Christ, there has never been any official formulation or unified consensus in orthodox Christianity of the mystery of the redemptive work of God in the sacrifice given in Jesus. Even though there is a consistency of imagery and language related to "sacrifice," there are a variety of emphases and interpretations throughout the tradition of Christian theology which carry equal weight and equal validity among Christians world-wide. [38]

It must be noted that Christian Tradition and its understanding of "sacrifice" is fundamentally rooted in the Jewish practice of sacrifice and atonement within the Hebrew Bible. Also, the experience of sacrificial rites in the major religions of the ancient world had a deep impact on Christian beginnings. "Sacrifices were the primary form of worship in Judaism from biblical times until the destruction of the Second Temple. Sacrifice was the dominant way of serving gods throughout the ancient Near East and was embraced by the Israelites as the means by which the people of YHVH could pay homage to the one God."[39] Animal sacrifices were the means by which the Jewish people expressed their faithfulness to God, who had been faithful to them. The practice of sacrifice was the liturgical expression of the Jewish people, and of individual Jews, of being in "right relationship with God."

In the 1st century, C.E., the Jewish sacrificial liturgical expression, which was the dominant theological point of view in Judaism at that time, took place in the Temple in Jerusalem. These sacrifices were prescribed in the Torah, and were an essential part of the religious understanding of every Jew. "These sacrifices of atonement (purification and reparation offerings) were necessitated by circumstances. Their purpose was to make reparation for sacrilege and to purge the divine abode of impurities and sins. Failing to offer them was held to be criminal. Public atonement sacrifices belonged to the yearly cycle of required offerings."[40] Through the killing of the animal in a sacrificial rite, an offering was made to purge the believer of sin and shame before God. "The need for such reconciliation is implicit in the Old Testament conception of God's absolute righteousness, to which nothing impure or sinful can approach. Its achievement is here represented as dependent on an act of God, whether by Divine appointment of the sacrificial system through which uncleanness, both ritual and moral, may be purged by the shedding of blood."[41] Thus, the emphasis upon sacrifice is related to purity and cleanliness, with a blood offering sacrifice being made to overcome our mortal limitations and failings so that we might be in "right relationship" with God.

Without doubt, the religious traditions of animal sacrifice, from which Jesus of Nazareth and the first followers of Jesus came, had an enormous impact upon the early church's understanding of why Jesus died on the cross. As the followers of Jesus began to formulate their self-understanding and their theological understandings as a community of faith, the images and theological categories of sacrificial worship, in full expression all around them in the ancient world, transferred easily to their experience and understanding of Jesus' life, death, and resurrection. We see this expressed by the early church in the language of the New Testament: While Jesus proclaimed the uselessness of blood-sacrifices considered as a substitute for repentance in some texts (Matthew 9:13), the early church has recorded in other verses Jesus as describing himself as "a ransom for many" (Mark 10:45). This language is continued in the institution of the Eucharist, where Jesus is said to have declared that the shedding of his blood constitutes a "New Covenant" for the "remission of sins." In St. John's Gospel, Jesus is described as "The Lamb of God who takes away the sin of the world," and his death is understood in a sacrificial light by being placed in juxtaposition to the sacrifice of the Paschal Lamb at the Passover. Thus, in the earliest Christian preaching, Jesus' death was already proclaimed to be a blood sacrifice "for our sins."[42] The Apostle Saint Paul continued the development of this theology of blood atonement, coming out of the tradition of blood sacrifice related to the Jewish Temple. For Saint Paul, "Christ's death and resurrection were the means by which we are redeemed from the effects of Law and its transgression, namely sin, from God's condemnation, and from death." [43] The peace made between God and humanity is made "through the blood of the cross" (Corinthians 1:20). In Saint Paul's language, blood sacrifice is a consistent image: The death of Christ was for Saint Paul an "expiation" for our sins (Romans 3:25). Elsewhere in the New Testament, the believer is said to be redeemed "with precious blood" (1 Peter 1:18), and the author of Hebrews makes constant use of sacrificial language in the same connection.[44] Aulen describes this as the earliest classical theory of atonement, where Christ is victorious over Satan, through his blood sacrifice on the cross.[45]

Thus, as the church moves out of the Apostolic Age, there is in place a strong emphasis upon sacrifice and blood atonement in the Christian Tradition. Of course, this is not the only theology of atonement present in the text or the early church. There is also in the New Testament, especially in the Synoptic Gospels, an emphasis upon a "kingdom of God" theology that expresses the atonement as a New Order, a New Creation being realized in the person of Jesus that is the kingdom of God, which is not necessarily dependant upon blood sacrifice. And, as these and other traditions exist side by side, often entwined together in the same proclamation, the church moved forward in time, with a theological richness that continued to develop. In the creedal traditions emerging out of this time period (such as the creedal hymn in Philippians 2:6-11), no theology of atonement finds singular expression. In each century, with new cultures and traditions of philosophy and social order impacting the church, new understandings of atonement were added into the theological conversation.

In the later Patristic Period, the theology of atonement was further developed by several contributors. The early Christian theologian Origen wrote that the death of Christ was the ransom paid to Satan, who had acquired rights over humanity by the

Fall, but was deceived into thinking he could hold the sinless Christ. Thus, God "tricked" Satan in the ransom death of Jesus. This position, with slight modifications, was held by a large number of influential church leaders, including St. Hilary of Poitiers, St. Augustine, and St. Leo. While maintaining that the devil had "rights" over sinful humanity, the exponents of this doctrine also commonly stressed that in trying to exercise these "rights" over the sinless Christ, Satan abused these "rights" and was thus conquered by the power of the resurrection.[46] Thus, in the Patristic Period, we can see the Church's understanding of the work of Jesus becoming more abstract and saturated with the mythological categories and theological understandings of the ancient world in which it existed.

Likewise, in the Middle-Ages, a shift in the dominant understanding of atonement took place which represented a theology born out of the social order of its day, that of Feudal Europe. In a mythology rooted in the social order of medieval Europe, St. Anselm wrote *Cur Deus Homo* [47], and his atonement theology of "satisfaction" and "substitution" emerged. For St. Anselm, the central role of Satan being defeated gave way to the central role of Jesus as substitute for humanity. "sin, being an infinite offence against God, required a satisfaction equally infinite. As no finite being, man or angel, could offer such satisfaction, it was necessary that an infinite being, i.e. God himself, should take the place of man, and by His death, make complete satisfaction to Divine Justice."[48] Thus, in this theology of atonement, Christ was not a ransom paid to the devil; instead, Christ was a debt paid to God, by God, in God's graceful plan that satisfied God's own demand for justice. St. Anselm's position became the dominant point of view, accepted with only few modifications by the Roman Church, and endorsed by such influential writers as St. Bernard and St. Aquinas with only moderate changes.

In the late Middle-Ages, a critic of Saint Anselm's Satisfaction Theory emerged: Peter Abelard, a 12th Century philosopher and theologian, rejected St. Anselm's view and refused to associate the death of Jesus with anything having to do with "the devil."[49]

"In his writings, he sought to prove the impossibility of the idea of "satisfaction," for if Adam's lesser fault required such a satisfaction, how much greater ought to be the satisfaction demanded by sins against Christ."[50] Thus, Abelard took a new direction. Abelard taught that the spiritual presence of Christ transformed the believer through grace. The believer was transformed and made one with God through the presence of Christ, the Teacher and Example. The presence and grace of Christ arouses a response of love and service in humanity; it is on this love which the basis of reconciliation between God and humanity rests. Abelard was certainly in the minority position in the Middle-Ages, and on through the Reformation. Yet his influence was felt, and Abelard's point of view was revived and built upon during the 19th century as more "modern" influences began to impact the church.

In the Reformation, the basic core of St. Anselm's position remained intact and dominant through both Catholic and Protestant traditions.

However, the Reformers gave new emphasis to the importance of "substitution." and developed what has been called the "Penal Theory" of atonement. Luther taught that Christ, in bearing by voluntary substitution the punishment due to man, was reckoned by God a sinner in his place. Calvin went even further in teaching that the Savior "bore in his soul the tortures of a condemned and ruined man." Jesus was a substitute, being punished in a blood sacrifice, for our sake, because of our sin, so that humanity would be in "right relationship" with God.

As the church moved forward into the Enlightenment, the influence of Rationalism began to take hold of the theological mind, especially in the circles of the Protestant church. When theologians began to consider the question of atonement, the earlier classical theories, saturated in the language and imagery of blood and sacrifice, were set aside. The culture of "modern" humanity was no longer in touch with the experience or mythology of blood sacrifice, either liturgically or culturally. Abelard's "subjective" theory of atonement, in opposition to St. Anselm, began to make more sense to the "modern" point of view. This "subjective" theory emphasized the love of Jesus, expressed in his life, death, and resurrection, as being the spiritual reality that brings us "at one" with God. We are called in this "moralistic" theory, to actualize this love of God in the world as a sign of our atonement. As Gustaf Aulen writes in *Christus Victor*:

> The humanizing theology of Liberal Protestantism, which is the background of the "subjective" view of the atonement, stood opposed in many ways to the scholastic theology which it challenged; but it fully accepted the rationalistic ideal. In its treatment of the atonement, it smoothes away all the oppositions with which the classic type abounds; all is made rationally clear; even the Love of God becomes rational. Further, it must be observed that this humanizing theology is penetrated from end to end by an idealistic philosophy, and seeks to interpret the Christian faith in the light of a monistic and evolutionary world view. [51]

However, the "subjective," rationalistic theory of atonement popularized by Liberal Protestantism is not without its faults. Serious questions have been raised regarding the "subjective" theory of atonement's weakness in confronting the reality of evil in this world. Often, the "rational" and "subjective" in a specific cultural setting can in fact be the dominant cultural assumptions held by the majority in power, which can often be oppressive and abusive to those in the minority, causing evil and injustice to abound. The "subjective" theory of atonement is just that: There is no firm stand against the presence of evil in our experience. This potentially makes the church and its proclamation a tool of the dominant cultural point of view, describing itself as "rational" and moral, and describing any minority point of view or community as less than valid or even labeled as "evil."

In his celebrated work, *Christus Victor*, Gustaf Aulen examines the three basic "Classic" theories of atonement listed above. In this work, Aulen takes a critical view of both St. Anselm's and

Abelard's positions. Aulen supports the earliest "classical" view of atonement, where Christ overcomes the mythological Satan, the hostile, evil powers that hold humanity in subjection and, at the same time, reconciles God to humanity. He sees this position as having prominence within the New Testament and reinterpreted for the modern world, is the most distinctly Christian idea that expresses the reality of atonement.[52]

A Critical Review of Atonement Theory: Violence/Nonviolence in Atonement

In the above history of the Classic theories of atonement, one contradiction comes forward again and again: Violence in the theology of atonement. How can the nonviolent Jesus do God's work of atonement through violent means? What is almost universally accepted is that Jesus of Nazareth lived and taught nonviolence. Further, the image and understanding of God taught by Jesus was profoundly nonviolent. Yet, when the church has historically attempted to interpret the meaning and purpose of the life of Jesus through theories of atonement, what is portrayed is a God of violence who kills his own "son" so that humanity might be saved. As we try to understand how the Tradition of Christian theology has related itself to gay and lesbian persons, it is important that we understand the relationship of violence to atonement theory. As J. Denny Weaver in his book *The Nonviolent Atonement* states: "Atonement theology starts with violence, namely the killing of Jesus. The commonplace assumption is that something good happened, namely the salvation of sinners, when or because Jesus was killed. It follows that the doctrine of atonement then explains how and why Christians believe that the death of Jesus – the killing of Jesus – resulted in the salvation of sinful humankind."[53]

This dominant view of atonement, that of the "Father" killing his "Son" for the redemption of the world, has had massive influence and implications in the history of Western Civilization. This dominant theory, set forth initially by St. Anselm, has influenced patterns of thinking in theology, politics, and jurisprudence. In the Western world, the prevailing theories of criminal justice have been significantly shaped by an ideology informed by the dominant atonement theories of the Church. This assumption is grounded in the belief that justice is gained and maintained by inflicting punishment, and that the greater the crime, the greater the punishment that should be applied. The correlation here to the teaching of the Church is that in the dominant classic atonement theory of the church, the sin (crimes) of humanity must be punished, and, because the sin is so deep and eternal, humanity cannot be punished enough. The only way that this sin can be justified is through the punishment of God's only Son, Jesus, as a substitute. Thus, a divine punishment, defined as the generosity and grace of God, is inflicted for an eternal crime. That is, sinful humanity can enjoy salvation because Jesus was killed in their place, satisfying the requirement of divine justice. This assumption, ideology, and theology has had an enormous impact. There is a pervasive use of violence in the criminal justice system when it operates on these shared beliefs. For example, an evil deed on one side must be balanced by an equivalent measure of violence on the other. This system, called retributive justice, is the dominant assumption found throughout the criminal justice system in the western world.

> The link between satisfaction atonement and systems of retributive justice cannot be denied. Timothy Gorringe's *God's Just Vengeance* provides a thorough analysis of satisfaction atonement's foundation in assumptions of retributive violence, as well as an extended discussion of the mutual interrelations between theories of satisfaction atonement and understandings of punishment and criminal justice in the western world since the time of Anselm. [54]

As we continue our discussion of the way in which Tradition in the church relates to gay and lesbian persons, we continue to see how the retributive justice ideology connected with the dominant theories of atonement in the life of the church have worked in cooperation in the oppression of homosexual people. One way to see this connection is to explore how other minority groups have also been affected by the violence implicit in classical atonement theology. I will review several critical assessments of classical atonement Theology, and afterward, explore how their experience shares great similarities with the experience of gay and lesbian people.

Other Points of View: Women and Ethnic Minorities

During the past century, a critical examination of the traditions of the church has emerged that has questioned many of the views long assumed true without question. The perspectives of women and ethnic minorities have been a refreshing and helpful lens through which to view the theology that has preceded us. Although many people view these perspectives with deep suspicion, when we open up our sensitivity to the voices of the marginalized, we gain a larger, clearer view of the world around us. If we listen, we hear the voices of women and ethnic minorities as the prophetic voice within the church today. These are the voices from the underside in Church Tradition. In my opinion, the church must come to terms with the reality that the dominant theologies handed down to us over the last millennium have been provided by people in places of power, in places of privilege, endorsed by rulers and principalities, and overwhelmingly male in perspective. The church began in the "margins" of society. For us to truly be connected to Jesus, we must consistently listen and heed the voices from the margins. If the church is to be the House of God for all people, we must reclaim our heritage; we must listen to the voices of the "marginal" and outcast today.

J. Denny Weaver agrees:

> Black, Feminist, and Womanist theologies have brought new questions to the atonement discussions in recent years. Each of these theologies is sensitive to earlier theological efforts to justify violence or oppression of women and people of color by appeal to the suffering of Jesus or the submission of Jesus to suffering required by a divine mandate. Consequently, Black and Feminist and Womanist voices have challenged any understanding of atonement that

presumes salvation or reconciliation to God that would understand the killing of Jesus as an act required in order to satisfy divine justice. [55]

Because violence has been the tool of the dominant against the poor and the oppressed, women and ethnic minorities, who historically have been the poor and the oppressed, have risen up to reject a theology of atonement which has violence, and submission to an authority who endorse violence, as the center of its teaching. It is helpful in our discussion of atonement as it relates to gay and lesbian people for us to look closely at the perspectives on atonement by representatives of other minority groups.

Black Theology

One great theologian who speaks directly to this is James Cone, author of *Black Theology* [56], and *God of the Oppressed* [57]. James Cone, an African-American theologian, writes that Black People and White People read history and tradition differently.

They focus on different agendas because of their different histories and different social location. Cone believes that the history of White Theology is primarily one of abstract systems built within their own logical patterns which posit ethereal solutions to theological problems such as predestination, free will, the existence of God, and structures of authority in the church. Likewise, White Theologians developed and endorsed an abstract system that expresses atonement through the substitution theory of St. Anselm, which places the primary meaning of salvation as taking place outside history. Cone describes White preaching and White Theology as defining Jesus as a "Spiritual Savior," who delivered people from "sin and guilt," with salvation largely being only a "spiritual" matter, separated from the concrete realities of the world.

In contrast to this, Black Theology, written from the experience of African and African-American perspectives, is a theology more rooted and grounded in history. It is more focused on the tasks of liberation, redemption, and reconciliation, which have their place in this world in concrete

experience: The God who liberates the Hebrews
from slavery; the God who pours out the Spirit on ***all
flesh***; the God who is known in the establishment of
a new reign of justice, righteousness, and peace.
When Black People read the Bible, they do not find
a docile Jesus politely teaching abstract theories,
they find Jesus the Liberator, working for justice,
calling forth liberation for all people against the
powers and principalities of this world.

Certainly, this difference of perspective is
found because of the different social location and
histories of Black verses White Christians. The
history of White Christianity has been, since the 4th
century, from a position of power and privilege. The
theologians who wrote from a European perspective
have been, for the most part, writers from within the
structures of Empire and power, not from the outside
or "underside" of the institutions of power. Black
Theology has been done from "the underside."
Black People and other people of color have written
their theology from the history of slavery,
oppression, racism, colonialism, and/or "Jim Crow"
segregation, issues which most White Theologians

have not taken the time nor developed the interest to understand, and certainly have not had the experience to reflect upon.

According to Cone, a "White" reading of the Bible focuses on the Christological formulations of Nicea, Chalcedon, and Anselm's Satisfaction theory. In light of this, Cone asks: "What are we to make of a tradition that investigated the meaning of Christ's relation to God and divine and human natures in his person, but failed to relate these Christological issues to the liberation of the slave and the poor in their society?"[58] According to Cone's analysis the church, and its interpreters, were thoroughly corrupted as vessels of the Roman State, and became the carriers of the values of Empire, rather than the liberating values and commitments of the Gospel of Jesus Christ. Thus, the church began to back away from a commitment to liberation and a struggle against oppression. [59]

> Few, if any, of the early Church
> Fathers grounded their
> Christological arguments in the
> concrete history of Jesus of
> Nazareth. Consequently, little is

said about the significance of his ministry to the poor as a definition of his person. The Nicene Fathers showed little interest in the Christological significance of Jesus' deeds for the humiliated, because most of the discussion took place in the social context of the church's position as the favored religion of the Roman State. [60]

Because of this way of doing theology, White Theologians could claim Jesus as defined by the abstract formulas of Nicea, Chalcedon, and St. Anselm's atonement theory, claiming to stand correctly in the orthodox tradition, but at the same time own slaves, continue to participate in the economic oppression of the poor, and endorse the violence of the state. In this way, the tradition of European theology separates itself from social ethics, as theology becomes an abstract language closed off from the real world of social consequence. The implications of Cone's critique for atonement theory are enormous. Cone focuses his critique on both St. Anselm, and Abelard: St. Anselm's view of atonement and salvation was built upon an assumption that salvation was summed up in a "spiritual transaction" done literally "out of this world," that had nothing to say about justice, righteousness, inclusiveness, and peace for the poor and oppressed. Such an atonement theory de-historicizes the work of Christ, separating it from God's liberating act in history.[61] It is not only St. Anselm's substitution theory that is criticized: For Abelard, Cone describes him as sentimentalizing the love of God into a subjective act of kindness and generosity, without the power to confront the very real, destructive power of evil and oppression in the world.[62]

Cone then reconstructs atonement as a "this world" reality where God is actively involved in history, in the midst of creation, seeking salvation, reconciliation, liberation, justice, peace, and inclusiveness for the poor, the helpless, and the oppressed. Cone, like Aulen, embraces the very earliest understanding of atonement expressed in the New Testament; however, Cone criticizes Aulen for expressing this atonement as "non-political" and instead proclaims a Risen Christ who is victorious in history against the evil powers of enslavement and destruction that operate in the social/political realm. According to Weaver, this is Cone's understanding of atonement: "The classical theory serves modern theology when it is radicalized politically, and liberation and reconciliation can be grounded in history and related to God's fight against he powers of enslavement. That is, the powers confronted and ultimately defeated by the resurrected Christ include not only the powers of evil mythically expressed in the figure of Satan, but earthly realities as well." [63]

The impact of Black Theology, represented here by James Cone, is devastating to the atonement theories inherited from Roman Empire and Euro-Protestant sources. From this perspective, we can see their failure: They are abstract, and conveniently separated from "this world" concerns. They are out of focus with the Social Gospel concerns of the poor, marginalized, and oppressed, and are compromised by their social location of complicity with the values and goals of the Imperial Powers from which they were produced.

In harmony with this critique is the point of view of Feminist and Womanist perspectives. In agreement with the above critique given by Black theologians, Feminist and Womanist voices add that the theologies inherited from European Christianity are profoundly male, profoundly distorted. Their criticism is that the point of view of White European theologies is from men, for men, without the perspective or input of women, and carry with them the values, assumptions, and goals embedded in an oppressive patriarchal world view (hierarchy, male privilege, submission of women to men, etc.), that do not accurately express the way of Jesus, nor the theology he proclaimed.

Feminist/Womanist Theologies

One of the great theologians to express this "Christian Feminism" is Rosemary Radford Ruether. In numerous books and articles, but most prominently in *Sexism And God-Talk*, Ruether offers a critique of the Christian faith handed down to us, and a reconstructed image and agenda of what Jesus, his movement, and the church should be about. In rejecting the classical theories of atonement, Ruether first offers her vision of the faith.[64] For her, the messianic mission of Jesus was about the coming Reign of God, with a specific emphasis upon the vindication of the poor, the marginalized, and the oppressed in a new reality of justice and peace for all people. Ruether sees the Jesus of the Gospels as one remarkably compatible with Feminism, in that Jesus spoke on behalf of marginalized and despised groups, including those people in the household of faith, and proclaiming God's love and hope for all people. Jesus rejected the idea of dominant-subordinate relations among social groups. Among leaders and followers, they were a community of equals. Women played important roles in Jesus' movement. In the earliest expressions of the movement women and men shared roles of power and prophesy unheard of in the religious communities of the ancient world. Jesus' vision of the vindication of the lowly in the breaking forth of God's new order was characterized by the breaking down of hierarchical caste privilege, and a nonviolent, active confrontation of the dominant powers of religion and government who were the instruments of oppression and empire in the social order. [65]

Within the spectrum of arguments found in Feminist literature, the issue of Jesus' maleness is important. The question remains: "Can a male savior save females?" Can Jesus, a male, be the atoning reality of God in the spiritual life of women, without sexism being present? Although there are different responses in the literature, those Feminists who call themselves Christian say that the maleness of Jesus has no ultimate significance, because in his life of seeking the liberation of humanity and uplifting of the oppressed and lowly, he announced and displayed a lifestyle that discards hierarchical privilege, rejects the oppression that builds up the patriarchal world, and proclaims the liberation of God. It is Jesus' humanity and his spirituality, not his gender, which is the central focus. [66]

In her specific rejection of classical theories of atonement, Ruether joins other Feminist, Womanist, and Black theologians in their critique: The arguments of St. Anselm, Abelard, and all those who appropriated their theories are caught up in an abstracted semantic exercise that uses patriarchal images portraying a "transaction" taking place in the spiritual realm, that not only has little to do with the "real world" history and proclamation of Jesus of Nazareth, but is also a damaging and destructive as a spiritual example, especially for women and minorities. In the classical theories of atonement, Jesus' death appears as a model of passive obedience to the Father's need to impose a mission of suffering and death. For Ruether, this entire image and agenda is rejected. Ruether argues that unjust or innocent suffering can never be redemptive or salvific. Jesus did not come to suffer and die; rather, Jesus came to liberate. The atonement we receive from the ministry of Jesus is the liberation and redemption realized in the Reign of God. In this, we know God and others in a beloved community and become one humanity, seeking what is just and right. While Jesus certainly realized that his mission and ministry would most certainly lead to his death, he did not come to die. Jesus came to proclaim life, conversion, healing, hope, peace, justice. In the death of Jesus, we see what should never happen: No one should suffer and die in oppression. In the death of Jesus, we see the oppression, abuse, and violence of the patriarchal powers in this world. The suffering and death of Jesus is not what is redemptive; rather,

suffering is the *risk* that one takes when one struggles to overcome unjust systems while seeking the redemption of God in the Reign of God. [67]

Another image that has become very important in the Christian Feminist critique of classical atonement theory is the image and issue of divinely sanctioned child abuse. Many Feminist theologians such as Ruether, Julie N. Hopkins, Rita Nakashima Brock, and others, focus on this important issue.[68] According to their point of view, the image of "the Father sending the Son to suffer and die for the sins of humanity" is nothing less than Divine-sanctioned child abuse. It is an image that says "suffering at the will of those who have authority over you" is redemptive. It is an image that says for a person to be of greatest value, they must sacrifice themselves. Thus, Divine child abuse is paraded as salvific and the child who suffers without even raising a voice is lauded as the hope of the world. Since women have been assigned the suffering-servant role in patriarchal societies, this worldview of divinely sanctioned, innocent suffering contributes to the victimization of women in both church and society. Thus, the images, roles, and theological agenda of classical atonement theory set women up to be victims of men in patriarchal society.

This image of God's abuse of His Son is found in every classical atonement theory: God hands over the Son to be killed by Satan, or to be killed by God's will, or as a moral example of the Suffering Servant. Suffering and abuse at the hands of the one in authority is an underlying value and assumption in every classical atonement theory, which defames all those who suffer needlessly and trivializes the tragedy of injustice.[69] Further, St. Anselm's view is that God's desire for justice is ***not*** that wrong should be righted, but that wrongs should be ***punished***. In St. Anselm's view, God's demand is that sin be punished; this punishment is laid upon

Jesus, because only Jesus can do it. Here, the message is that punishment and abuse is the very nature of God. Julie N. Hopkins adds, "A god who punished through pain, despair, and violent death is not a god of love but a sadist and despot." [70] In the argument of Christian Feminists, the image and concept of "God delivering Jesus to be killed" is almost universally rejected.

In unison with Black and Feminist theologians, Womanist theology rejects the images and assumptions found in the classical theories of atonement. However, the voice of Black Women (Womanist) sometimes takes a different track from other liberation theologies. The Womanist theologian points out that Feminist theologians have assumed that the experience of White women is normative for all women. In consequence, Womanist theologians, such as Delores Williams and Katie Cannon, charge that Feminist theology has ignored the differences between White women and women of color. [71]

One of the most powerful voices in Womanist theology is Delores Williams. In her work, she identifies the role of "surrogate" as the role often played by Black women in White patriarchal society. The surrogate is the individual who is lowest on the hierarchical scale, who "stands in" for others in roles of servitude, such as cook, maid, and "mammy." The surrogate does the dirty work others will not do, and is exploited personally, economically, and spiritually. In the modern context, the surrogate is also the person who is the "token," the person or employee who is placed in a position to satisfy some legal requirement, not hired out of genuine value for them as a human being.

For Delores Williams, classical theories of atonement present Jesus as the ultimate "surrogate" figure. Jesus is exploited by God so that humanity can reap the benefit. Williams states: "If Black women accept this idea of surrogate redemption, can they not also passively accept the exploitation that surrogacy brings?" [72]

> We must show that redemption of
> humans can have nothing to do

with any kind of surrogate or
substitute role Jesus was reputed to
have played in a bloody act that
supposedly gained victory over sin
and/or evil… Rather, it seems more
intelligent and more scriptural to
understand that redemption had to
do with God, through Jesus, giving
humankind a new vision to see the
resources for positive, abundant
relational life. [73]

In Williams' atonement theology, the image of Jesus
on the cross is the image of human sin, of
defilement, a gross manifestation of collective
human sin. Clearly it was the manifestation of evil
that was responsible for the death of Jesus, not God.
[74]

In Womanist understanding, Jesus does not
passively submit to unjust suffering. Jesus actively
confronts it in life-giving ministry. The activist
rather than passive mode is very significant. Victims
are passive. Victims can only submit. To resist evil
and oppression is to cease being a passive
victim/surrogate, even if suffering is the result. Yet,
the suffering that will come from seeking justice and

righteousness is *not* salvific, although it is the price that has to be paid in resistance. Resisting is the beginning of accepting responsibility rather than merely accepting abuse.[75] It is in the church's activist ministry that we experience the presence of the Risen Christ, and in this struggle for peace, justice, reconciliation, and righteousness we experience the atonement God yearns for us. It is the seeking of God's Reign that is salvific, not the suffering that comes with it.

Pacifist Theology

One additional point of view related to the tradition of atonement theory is the point of view found in the radical reformation among many within the Anabaptist/Mennonite tradition. While certainly being in the minority, there were significant voices in that movement that made the critical connection between the institutional violence found in the established churches of Rome and England, and the violence also found in the atonement theologies handed down by these institutions.[76] These radical reformation traditions, in their separation from the dominant traditions of the Roman and British Empire, proclaimed a pacifism which critically questioned any use or endorsement of violence in the Christian faith.

J. Denny Weaver, in his book, *The Nonviolent Atonement*, sets forth a persuasive argument for a new understanding of the atonement from a pacifist, nonviolent position. Weaver asks the simple question of how can a movement based upon a prophet who proclaimed nonviolence be associated with atonement theories which present the God, whom Jesus represents, as bringing forth salvation through the violent means of killing Jesus on the cross? Weaver rejects the dominant classical theories of atonement, and constructs a new theory called "Narrative Christus Victor." In Narrative Christus Victor, the oldest theory described by Aulen, and the theory most prominent in the New Testament, is reinterpreted to describe the atonement of Christ as not being accomplished by the violence of the cross, but through the prophetic witness of the ministry of Jesus, and the power of the resurrection.[77] *Narrative Christus Victor* embraces the "narrative" form of the New Testament witness, but demythologizes the concept of Jesus Christ overcoming the mythological figure of Satan. Instead, Jesus Christ confronted the "Powers and Principalities" of this world with the new reality of the Reign of God. Even though these "Powers and Principalities" killed Jesus, God, through the power of the resurrection, has redeemed all of creation, confirming for us the way of Jesus as God's hope and salvation for the world.

What Does This Mean For Gay and Lesbian People?

As I began this chapter, the question was, "What do these theories of atonement mean for homosexual people?" What are the underlying assumptions, consequences, and implications of these theories for this community of people who are very much on the margins of church and society? My opinion is that the classical theories of St. Anselm and Abelard are destructive and harmful, not only to the church in general, but especially to minority groups within the church, and most especially to homosexual persons. In unison with Black, Feminist, Womanist, and Pacifist perspectives I see these classical atonement theories as abstract theories, conveniently separated from "this world" concerns, out of focus with the Social Gospel concerns of the poor, marginalized, and oppressed. These Classic theories are compromised by their social location of complicity with the values and goals of the violence of the Roman Empire and other Empires, powers and principalities from which they were produced. I agree with the summary in J. Denny Weaver's *The Nonviolent Atonement*:

> The conclusion is inescapable that satisfaction atonement is based on divinely sanctioned, retributive violence. The various arguments that add additional biblical images, redefine punishment, point to other emphases, appeal to the Trinity, or emphasize that the Father bears the suffering with the Son serve to mitigate or camouflage but do not alter the underlying presupposition that satisfaction depends on a divinely sanctioned death so that

which is necessary to satisfy the
offended divine entity, whether
God or God's law or God's honor.
Satisfaction atonement depends on
the assumption that doing justice
means to punish, that a wrong deed
is balanced by violence. The
attempts to refurbish Anselm blunt
the edges of the offending violence
but do not eliminate it. Anyone
uncomfortable with the idea of a
God who sanctions violence, a God
who sends the Son so that at his
death can satisfy a divine
requirement, should abandon
satisfaction and Anselmian
atonement forthwith. [78]

For gay and lesbian people, the impact of this
theology of violence and abuse has borne horrific
consequences. First, the Satisfaction Theory of
atonement separates the person of Jesus from his
prophetic role of Liberator and Emancipator. It sets
up an abstract theory of divine transaction as the
center of salvation and minimizes the prophetic
witness of Jesus for justice, hospitality,
reconciliation, and nonviolence for all people,
especially people who are on the margins of society.

In doing this, minority groups, especially sexual minority groups, are easily, conveniently disenfranchised from their participation in the community of the church, because the prophetic voice that urges inclusive hospitality toward the stranger is subdued or silenced. Instead, in classical atonement theory, the action of violence and punishment takes center stage. In a religious system based on violence toward an offending party, the pattern of scapegoating, blame, and harassment of people in minority social groups soon become central to the social order of church and society.

Scapegoating is especially relevant. Scapegoating, the act of holding a person, group of people, or institution responsible for the problems of society, is rampant for homosexual people. In very recent years, we have heard many voices of the Religious Right such as Jerry Falwell, James Dobson, and many others, scapegoat homosexual people and blame them for everything from the horrors of AIDS, the terrorist attacks of 9/11, to the destruction of Hurricane Katrina. Those of us familiar with the theories of Christian anthropologist

Rene Girard, can see how these patterns of violence, punishment, and the scapegoat of the minority can become a powerful, violent force in society.[79]

Girard has provided a helpful construction of the scapegoat theory. In Girard's view, humankind is violent. Humans are driven by desire for that which another person has or wants (mimetic desire). This desire causes a triangulation of desire, where multiple people (or groups of people) are directly competing for the same object or position in society. This situation results in conflict among the desiring parties which threatens the function of the society. This mimetic contagion increases to a point where society is at risk. It is at this point that the scapegoat mechanism is triggered. This is the point where one person or one group is singled out as the cause of the trouble and is expelled or killed by the dominant group to supposedly make society acceptable for everyone else. This person or group that is abused is the scapegoat. For the dominant group, social "order" is restored as people are contented that they have solved the cause of their problems by removing the scapegoat, and the cycle begins again. Using

Girard's theory, we can see how the dominant theories of atonement in the Christian church have been used ideologically to marginalize gay and lesbian people (as well as other minorities), and "set them up" to be punished as the scapegoat. They are "punished" because they are labeled as a "threat" to society.

It is clear from the work of Timothy Gorringe, in *God's Just Vengeance: Crime, Violence, and the Rhetoric of Salvation,* that a society whose religious point of view is endorsement of violent punishment for sins which have been committed, has an inevitable movement towards violence and punishment for all who are on the margins of society. [80] Groups that are outside the norm are abused or "punished" through the scapegoating process. The effect of this religious/social world view upon the United States is profound. Today, a larger percentage of the population of our country is imprisoned than in any time in recorded history, and sexual minorities are punished severely, scapegoated in both legally and non-legally sanctioned ways in church and society.

A Nonviolent Theology of Atonement For All People

Atonement is the understanding of how our relationship with God and each other can be redeemed and reconciled so that we are "At One." How can the church be reconciled to homosexual persons? How are all of us, together, reconciled to God? The church must affirm a theology of atonement that proclaims the hospitality of Christ for all people. It must not be an atonement theory based upon violence, death, and punishment. The church today must have a theory of atonement that focuses on the prophetic witness of Jesus Christ urging hospitality, forgiveness, reconciliation, justice, nonviolence, and new life for *all* people. For homosexual persons to be welcomed and affirmed in the life of the church, we must come to a new understanding of atonement in the Christian life. The first step toward this atonement and reconciliation is an acknowledgement that the current dominant classical theology of atonement is a barrier unto itself: The classical theories of atonement we currently embrace do not work. They do not "carry the faith." Just as Jesus "Cleansed the Temple" as a way of demonstrating that the theological status-quo of the religious establishment of his day was obsolete, we must do the same with the classic theories of atonement, so that we can proclaim the hospitality of Jesus to *all* people, especially the marginalized and oppressed communities in our midst.

Most refreshing and inspiring is the model of atonement set forth in J. Denny Weaver's *The Nonviolent Atonement.* It is a theory of atonement that is rooted in the historic authorities of the faith and informed by a wide spectrum of theological opinion and dialogue. I will close this chapter with a quotation from his conclusion:

> Abandoning Anselm is not to challenge Jesus as Savior, nor to abandon the salvific work of Jesus. Abandoning satisfaction atonement is to challenge one way of talking about *how* Jesus saves. The challenge pointed out is the

multiple ways in which this particular explanation of the *how* of Jesus' saving work is linked to violence in some form. Proposing Narrative Christus Victor as an alternative to satisfaction atonement is to propose a *how* explanation that focuses on Jesus life as the reign of God rather than on Jesus' death as the act of God. Narrative Christus Victor is a biblical way of understanding the salvific work of Jesus without imaging God as one who abuses the perfect Son for the benefit of others. The God of Narrative Christus Victor does suffer with Jesus in making the reign of God visible in the world. But this suffering was not the specific purpose of Jesus' mission, nor was it required by a divine equation. [81]

CHAPTER 3:

REASON

Simon was born into a working-class African-American family who lived in a large southern city in the United States. As a child, Simon began acting "girly" to his friends and siblings. Simon's effeminate behavior was a great embarrassment and shame to his father. His father began beating Simon whenever he behaved "like a girl." As Simon grew up, it became evident that he was very talented as a musician. Simon wrote songs, and began associating with other musicians who taught him how to operate recording equipment. Simon eventually became proficient at this and worked in radio broadcasting. During this time, Simon was estranged from his father, who "swore he never wanted to see me again." Simon was gay, and displayed his sexual orientation quite openly. Simon then moved to a large city in the western USA, where he also worked in radio broadcasting. Simon began using illegal drugs, and eventually became addicted to drugs, which destroyed his life. Simon was arrested, charged, and convicted of being a drug dealer, and was sent to state prison. While in prison, Simon was beaten to the very point of death, but survived. The injuries he sustained to his head from this beating left Simon mentally incapacitated and handicapped. Simon was released from prison and sent back to his parents in his home town, who received a disability check each month to assist them in caring for him. However, Simon was not welcomed into the house where his father lived. Simon, unable to live at home and unable to maintain a residence for himself, began living on the streets of the city. His parents occasionally would stop by on the street and give him money. There on the streets, Simon would write and sing songs, beg for money, and regularly get in fist fights with people who did not appreciate his talent. Simon was a very well dressed man. He would sort through the "clothes closet" of the local mission church and find the most colorful, vibrant clothing available, and make for himself very noticeable, attractive attire. Simon died of an undisclosed illness in the fall of 2008. He was a gifted, talented gay man, abandoned by his family and left to live homeless on the street because he was a homosexual.

Reason is defined as an authority in that it is the dispassionate analysis of data, evidence, theory from critical philosophical thought and scientific exploration. In the Anglican and Wesleyan tradition, we are "Children of the Enlightenment," carrying with us assumptions about the value and importance of the scientific method, embracing the discoveries of science and its critical study as the search for truth: All truth is God's truth; thus, reason and science are our allies in the greater understanding of God's good creation. It is of vital importance that we define our understanding of humanity, sexuality, and homosexual persons through a dialogue with the reasoned consensus of the scientific/medical community, not ignoring or dismissing what has been discovered through rigorous scientific study. I find it tragically painful that some Christians within our churches embrace the discoveries of science and reasoned study when it applies to cancer, heart disease, and mental illness, quickly traveling to their physician or hospital (the "temple" of reason and science) when science benefits them individually, then turn around and refuse to let the careful, reasoned scientific study of sexuality and homosexuality impact their assumptions and bias related to homosexual persons.

The Reality of Sexuality

It is an indisputable fact that a part of humankind is primarily or exclusively homosexual, sexually oriented toward persons of the same sex. Studies done over the past three decades conclude that approximately 5 to 7 percent of all people studied are homosexual.[82] However, there is no agreement as to why this is the case. While it is not relevant or even possible to examine all the varied arguments about the origins of homosexuality in this report, a brief survey of the most recent and influential scientific explanations of homosexuality would be helpful.

Modern interpretations of the reasons for and manifestations of what is called homosexuality are quite scattered. Explanations offered by various studies correspond with the formulations of problems and methods of particular disciplines. For example, the approach and questions of a psychiatrist, a genetic specialist, and a sociologist differ considerably from one another, and the weight of each scientific explanation of homosexuality can be evaluated differently within the boundaries of each particular model and discipline of interpretation. Further complications are caused by the fact that existing attitudes and passions often determine the ways questions are posed and tend to serve the ends of various sexual and gender politics…at least this is what scholars from different fields accuse each other of doing. And, the question arises whether a value-free approach to the study of sexuality can ever be possible.[83] Thus, a unified multi-disciplinary scientific explanation for the causes of homosexuality is not present.

It is also important to note that any study of homosexuality must be done in the full context of heterosexuality, and of sexuality in general. It would be more accurate to say that any study of homosexuality is one in the same as a study of heterosexuality: One cannot be understood separate from the other. And, in all studies of sexuality, for homosexual as well as heterosexual people, we seem to have more questions that we do answers.

In the sciences of psychology and psychiatry, there was considerable debate during the 20th century about the origins of homosexuality. In traditional, conservative Freudian Theory, the presence of homosexuality is an abnormal development related to an unresolved Oedipal conflict in which a child has an unhealthy attachment to the mother. However, most modern Freudian therapists reject this 19th century point of view. For Behavioral and Social Scientists, and Anthropologists, there was in the beginning a stress on "learning" and environmental factors. Some pointed to childhood experiences of undefined gender roles in the family. Most of these explanations have been hotly debated and are now looked upon with suspicion by most mental health professionals. [84]

Other scholars have tried to explain homosexuality biologically as related hormones, genes, and their impact upon the brain. Research on the relative amount androgens and estrogens in homosexuals and heterosexuals has produced contradictory results. In spite of efforts to find a genetic origin of sexuality, scholars have not yet been able to find a gene that would explain homosexuality as a purely hereditary phenomenon. However, some recent studies indicate that the sexual orientation of some male homosexuals might be determined by their chromosomes. [85]

In general, the research on same-sex orientation and sexual relations has been characterized by the traditional distinction between "nature" versus "nurture." In light of the failure to discover a unified understanding of the origins of human sexuality, this dichotomy, this point of view, has been roundly criticized in recent literature as simplistic and not descriptive of human sexuality.[86] It seems that human sexuality is not "either/or;" it appears to be "both/and." In the early 1990's, while working on The Committee to Study Homosexuality of the United Methodist Church, one of my fellow Committee members, Dr. Tex Sample, Professor of Christian Ethics at St. Paul School of Theology in Kansas City, MO, commented on the lack of certainty related to the scientific study of human sexuality: "Maybe in twenty years we will learn more about it; maybe there will be a greater understanding in the future. Coming into this study, I thought that science would provide clearer insight. I thought that we would find some consensus of certainty about what causes homosexuality. However, that is not the case. Now, it seems we must rely on other ways of knowing and understanding." [87]

However, in spite of the differences of opinion regarding the origins of homosexuality, there *is* much that can be reliably demonstrated about how homosexual people behave in society, and how they relate to one another as a minority. As we move into the 21st century, the overwhelming body of evidence from the study of social science is that homosexuality is no more destructive to a person than being heterosexual. The scientific data shows that gay and lesbian people are no more likely than heterosexual people to be prone to mental illness, criminal behavior, or sexual abuse. Every medical/scientific professional organization representing the mainstream and consensus of the medical/scientific community has rejected a "negative" understanding of homosexuality or homosexual persons: The American Psychological Association, The American Psychiatric Association, The American Pediatric Association, and The American Medical Association do not list homosexuality as a mental illness nor as socially maladaptive behavior. Their consensus, established over 30 years ago, has not been challenged; rather, it has grown into an overwhelming consensus within the medical/scientific community, that homosexuality is no more nor less healthy than heterosexuality. [88] Further support for this position is found in that child-welfare organizations "support the parenting of children by lesbians and gay men, and condemn attempts to restrict competent, caring adults from serving as foster and/or adoptive parents." [89] Such organizations include the Child Welfare League of America, North American Council on Adoptable Children, American Academy of Pediatrics, American Psychiatric Association, American Psychological Association, and the National Association of Social Workers. On July 28, 2004, the American Psychological Association's Council of Representatives adopted a resolution supporting legalization of same-sex civil marriages and opposes discrimination against lesbian and gay parents.

This is what I discovered as a member of the United Methodist Committee to Study Homosexuality, and what I have observed as a pastor who has studied, researched, and struggled in prayerful discernment: The overwhelming evidence from the vast majority of research in every discipline I have studied is that gay and lesbian sexual orientation is rarely, if ever, a conscious "lifestyle" chosen. From the results of diligent study, it is apparent to me that the sexual orientation of gay and lesbian people is who they are at the very core of their sense of self: Homosexual people are made who they are in the same physiological and psychological way that heterosexual people are made. The evidence demonstrates that sexual orientation, both homosexual and heterosexual, is set extremely early in one's life, and is very difficult, if not virtually impossible to change.[90] I ask you: When did you *decide* to become a heterosexual or homosexual? Why would anyone *choose* to be a part of an oppressed, abused, and condemned minority?

Further, longitudinal studies clearly demonstrate that those who seek through counseling to "change" their sexual orientation fail. People can, through guilt and shame, change their *behavior* over short periods of time, but their sexual ***orientation*** remains the same. Homosexual people can pretend to be heterosexual; they can conform to personal/social/religious pressure and alter their behavior. However, the overwhelming evidence shows that sexual orientation is as firmly set as the color of ones' eyes, or whether one is right-handed or left-handed.[91] It would be just as difficult for a heterosexual to change into being a homosexual, as it would for a homosexual to change into being a heterosexual.

The definition of homosexuality as a ***neutral*** rather than a destructive or ***negative*** category within human diversity has a profound impact upon our evaluation of sexuality. Homosexuality is "neutral" in that a gay person, like a heterosexual person, has the full capacity and potential to think, choose, feel, and respond in a healthy, mature, adult manner to the moral, ethical, relational demands of life. How then can the church or society label homosexuality as destructive or maladaptive when all of the assumptions about its supposed destructive or maladaptive nature are refuted by sound, reasonable, reliable study? It is fundamentally apparent that homosexual people, like heterosexual persons, are not *inherently* destructive, abusive, nor damaging to themselves or others. It cannot be demonstrated that to be gay is to be contrary to the common good of society. Apart from a narrow, literalistic interpretation of a handful of Biblical texts, there is simply no evidence or justification for defining homosexuality as inherently negative or destructive. The overwhelming majority of gay and lesbian persons, like heterosexual persons, lead normal, healthy, productive, moral lives. They are in our schools, in our communities as responsible citizens, in our churches as faithful members, and are honorable in their relationships with others. [92]

Conservatives or "Traditionalists," in commenting on the reality of homosexuality, often say that this movement of tolerance and hospitality to homosexual persons represents a "decline in the moral standards" of society, a decline in the influence of the church and its ethical teachings, and "a turning of a blind eye to sin."

I do not believe this is true. What is actually happening is that persons in church and society are realizing that their homosexual family members, neighbors, and church members are just as capable of living moral, ethical, responsible lives as heterosexual persons. Further, persons who are compassionate to the experience of minorities, open to the diversity within human culture, and perceptive of the abuse and oppression experienced by gay and lesbian persons, are now aware that it is **homophobia** and its oppression that is the destructive behavior, not homosexuality. [93]

Certainly, one could produce evidence of anti-social behavior or destructive behavior in the gay community. Certainly, one could document case studies of pathological, maladaptive men and women in the gay community. Yes, it is easy to do this, just as it is easy to produce the same evidence of pathology and destructive behavior of persons in the heterosexual majority. If one were searching diligently to attack the gay community, one might even hide the issue of sexual orientation behind the image of a sexually abused young person who was forced to participate in gay sex through the torture of a dominant partner, and in such a relationship the abused youth supposedly "became" gay. Yes, one could produce this sort of "evidence," ignoring or masking the reality that in such cases, the presenting and central issue is the *abuse* to the victim, not the person's sexual behavior or orientation. Sexual abuse is to be condemned regardless of the context. And such cases of abuse, whether homosexual or heterosexual, leave deep and life-long scars profoundly affecting the sexual life and sexual experience of those abused. However, in such horrific cases, the issue is not one's sexual identity or orientation; the issue is the abuse. Also, such "case studies" represent only an extremely tiny percentage of persons who could be categorized as "gay" and in no way represent the overwhelming majority of gay and lesbian persons in society who know themselves to be homosexual without experiencing any such abuse or negative influence.

I include this analysis of abuse vs. orientation here because I recently sat in the office of a Bishop and discussed the issue of homosexuality. This

Bishop actually referenced this dynamic of abuse and young persons being "forced" or influenced to "become gay" as one of his arguments for resisting full hospitality and welcome to gay and lesbian persons in the life of the church. It is a sad reality that minority groups are often judged and labeled by the extreme actions of their most outrageous and destructive members. Nowhere is this bigotry more true than our society's stereotype of homosexual persons. I believe that our "heterosexual world" has endorsed a distorted stereotype of gay and lesbian people of rampant promiscuity and irresponsible sexual behavior which is false, and blinds us to the truth of who the vast majority of gay and lesbian people really are. Gay and lesbian people are really just like the rest of us. Certainly, the most important aspect for me in the ministry of the church is how I know and relate to homosexual people whom I encounter. The overwhelming majority of homosexual persons I know lead normal, healthy, productive, moral lives.

As we step back and take in the view of the *neutral* identity that homosexuality now holds within the medical, scientific, and mental health communities, what does that mean for us in the religious community, especially the Christian faith? It seems to me that the assumptions long held by Christians that homosexuality is a "sickness" or "sin" must be challenged and identified as bias and bigotry. It is my experience that this label of "sick" is almost directly translated as a second label of "sin" by most members of the churches I have served. Theologically, ethically, sin is that which is contrary to the will of God, that which is destructive of God's good purpose in this world. Since it can be clearly demonstrated through diligent scientific research and study from multiple disciplines that homosexuality is not inherently destructive to individuals and society, how can anyone in the church justify any definition of homosexuality as a "sick" or "sinful?" It seems to me that the church should not reject gay and lesbian people as "incompatible" or sinful. The church should confess its sin of homophobia and seek to be reconciled with the millions of people it has abused. The church should then defend homosexual people as God's good creation and full members of the Body of Christ.

CHAPTER 4:

EXPERIENCE

John was born into a faithful, devoted Christian family that never missed a Sunday in church. He was raised in his small town's largest United Methodist congregation. John's family was very conservative, both politically and theologically. John's family was hard working farmers who lived in the country, far away from the hustle and bustle of big city life. John's father was the "strong, silent type" who spoke more with his work and his actions than he did with his words. John knew he was different, but couldn't exactly tell why until he was older. He didn't fit in with what most everyone else said was normal. John knew from an early age he was attracted to men instead of women. He knew this, but he didn't talk about it because he understood that it wasn't normal. John broke with family tradition and told his parents that he wanted to go to college down at the state capitol, in the big city. He didn't want to be a farmer. John went off to college, and there in school slowly began to identify himself with the gay community on campus. John kept this association to himself and did not speak to his parents or anyone else from his past about his homosexuality. Finally, as John prepared to graduate from college, he decided that he did not want to continue living a lie to his parents. He wanted to be honest with them about his life. John went home with the intention of telling his parents that he was gay. John first told his father that he was gay. John sat down at the kitchen table with him and told him that he had known since he was a little boy that he was gay, and that he did not want to hide it from him any longer. John's father got up from the table and went into his bedroom and brought back to the kitchen table a pistol. John's father laid the pistol on the table and told his son that he should never tell his mother what he had just told him, and that he knew what he was supposed to do with this gun. John was stunned beyond belief by what his father had just said and done. John immediately left and never returned home.

Experience As Authority

In the Wesleyan Tradition, experience is an authority in our Christian faith. It is the experience of the Holy Spirit that is most significant. How we experience the Holy Spirit around us, how we incorporate the rich and diverse interactions of our experienced world, in individual and social relationships, profoundly impacts how we understand and relate to God, to human institutions, to other individuals, and with the natural world. Experience is an authority because it shapes us. Just as Scripture shapes us, just as tradition shapes us, just as reason shapes us, our experience throughout time shapes us to the core of our being. Whereas Scripture, tradition, and reason are more "codified" references, which have been "objectified" through the dogmatic lens of the religious and secular institutions that surround us, experience is the received feed of data, emotion, interaction, and reflection that is filtered through our own personal, interpersonal, and cultural filters, where we "make sense of it all" in the situations encountered throughout time. Experience is our "context" where we receive and relate multiple points of view, all competing for our allegiance and choices. Out of this interaction, our experience forms within us questions and conflicts, and each of us struggles to "makes sense" of this experience within the vessel of our inherited religious and cultural point of view and traditions.

Experience is the fertile ground out of which grew the other three authorities of the faith in the Wesleyan Tradition: It is the experience of the Holy Spirit that both produced and "makes sense" out of the witness of Scripture. It is experience that sorts through tradition. It is experience that critically examines what has been established as reason in our cultural, scientific, and religious understanding. What is Scripture but the preserved and written down foundational experiences of those in the faith who have gone before us? What is tradition but the experiences of the faithful preserved through the ages, as they worked, worshiped, studied, and struggled with their faith? What is reason but the careful analysis of believers, put to the critical test of their faith seeking understanding?

Experience is where we interact with the mystery we call the Holy Spirit. Each person encounters the mystical, spiritual presence of God in the context of a religious community and culture, and we must shape for ourselves the meaning and purpose that the Holy Spirit produces out of that experience. It is the Biblical witness that the Holy Spirit is active and vibrant in the community of faith pouring out gifts to each person and within the congregation at large. According to 1 Corinthians, chapters 12 & 13, the Holy Spirit gives gifts of love, faith, hope, wisdom, knowledge, discernment, prophecy, healing, the ability to speak languages, and the ability to interpret languages. In Galatians, chapter five, St. Paul tells us that the Holy Spirit produces "fruits" in the life of individuals and the congregation at large. The "fruits" of the Holy Spirit are love, joy, peace, patience, kindness, generosity, faithfulness, gentleness, and self-control. Each person must encounter the Holy Spirit with other people in the context of their community and culture, and shape for themselves a relationship with others that is in continuity with the call and movement of the Holy Spirit in their own lives. All of this is done in the context of our faith, in relationship with other Christians, past and present, seen through the lens of all of the authorities of the faith, in concert together, moving forward toward the future. In the Wesleyan tradition, it is the Holy Spirit that leads us in the interpretation of Scripture, tradition, reason, and experience, and it is the Holy Spirit that moves us forward in faith as we encounter the challenges of our common life, making our faith a living faith, rather than a mere history of what has been. Bound up within the movement of history, the authorities of our faith are imperfect guides in need of the movement and work of the Holy Spirit within the discerning community of the church to give us clarity and direction.

Some might ask: "If the authorities of our faith are limited by their historical and cultural particularities, how can they be truly authoritative in our life and faith?" For me, the authorities of our faith maintain their power and place as authorities because they are affirmed and lived out in the context of a loving, thought-filled, prayer-filled, worshiping community of faith that is alive in the Holy Spirit, carefully interpreting the reality of all of these authorities (Scripture, Tradition, Reason, and Experience) in a balanced, self-critical, faithful dialogue which encounters the past, present, and future in the light of these multiple witnesses of faith. It is the community of faith, the shared, living reality of the church, which makes real and firm these authorities in our life as we move together in the Spirit.

All of this is the context and meaning of experience as an authority: Our experience is the "primordial soup" out of which all authority in the faith comes forth, grows, and becomes what it is. Think for a moment about the context of the earliest days of the Christian experience: Before the New Testament was written, before the ecclesial hierarchy of the Church formed, before the great works of Christian theology were begun, it was the *experience* of the risen Jesus, the *experience* of the Holy Spirit, and the *experience* of lives changed because of these revelatory events, all in the context of their received Judeo/Greco/Roman culture, which made possible the beginnings of a church that has continued and led us to where we are today. This experience was and is grounded and rooted in the proclamation of the Reign of God in Jesus Christ both within the Jewish culture where it was formed, and against the cultural experience of history. This Reign of God experienced in Jesus Christ is the arrival of peace with justice, forgiveness and reconciliation, new life and eternal life in a walk of discipleship in a community of faith open to all people in all of our contexts. And it has been the experience of these realities continually in the life of the Church which has brought forth all of the authorities of our faith, which continue to lead us forward as we interpret our faith.

As an authority, we trust our experience of the Holy Spirit in the life of the church to move us forward in faith. It illumines our understanding of God and creation, and motivates us to make sensitive moral judgments. Some facets of human experience tax our theological understanding. The pain of our experience is a great burden: Many people live in terror, hunger, loneliness, and oppression. Everyday experiences of birth and death, of growth and life in the created world, and an awareness of our wider social experiences belong to serious theological reflection and impact how we interpret the authorities of faith. Certainly, our 21st century context of cultural conflict and debate about sexuality brings forth many stories of pain and hardship for us all, and demand honest theological reflection within the community of faith. We trust the Holy Spirit to lead us.

In relation to sexuality, how have you experienced your own sexual journey? How have you experienced shame, avoidance, ignorance, and silence in relation to many issues of sexuality as an individual in our culture, especially related to homosexuality? How have you experienced the silence and avoidance of homosexuality in your family? A simple awareness of the reality that at least 5 to 7 percent of the population is homosexual means that close to you, in your family or your church, there are homosexual persons. Are you aware of them? How have they been treated? How have they been silenced? Are they "in the closet?" How have they been shamed, shunned, or quietly "driven away?" How has the experience of rejection in family, church, and society affected them? Oppressed them? Humiliated them? When has hatred and violence, either physical or verbal, towards homosexual persons erupted in your life? Toward you? In your community? In your church? How has this hatred and violence affected homosexual persons and their families? Reflection upon this experience of exclusion and abuse of gay and lesbian people opens the door to often ignored and avoided realities associated with how homosexual persons experience our world and church. Reflect upon how homosexual persons have experienced God in the context of a church that rejects their very identity as "incompatible with Christian teaching." How have you experienced gay and lesbian people as full of the gifts of the Holy Spirit? How have you experienced homosexual people at work in the church in evidence of their "fruits" of the Holy Spirit? How does our experience of the Holy Spirit lead us to respond? Experience is an authority in our faith, when it is guided by the Holy Spirit.

Experience as Interpretation

Experience is the task of interpretation. Everything is interpreted. There are no experiences that are not subjectively understood and cognitively sorted through in the particularities of our human limitations. Complete objectivity, even when related to the authorities of our faith, is not possible. Our experience is mediated and interpreted, through the many variables of culture, social location, religious assumptions, and personal values. In many ways these variables are dependent upon our own individual histories and choices. In other ways, these variables are determined by our location in the context of culture, history, and time.

Even those things most sacred to us, such as Scripture and tradition, are "caught" in the particularities of human existence, and must be interpreted as they are defined in the context of time and human understanding. Further, how we encounter these realities which are sacred to us is conditioned by the interpretations we bring to them. For example, there is no "face value" or "value free" interpretation of a text: We bring to the task of interpretation our own assumptions, values, histories, and prejudices to the text, which "color" and direct our trajectories of how it is understood.

Let me give you an example of how this "web" of particularities applies to me: I am a white male, which places me in the dominant racial group and the dominant gender group in my society. I am in my late 40's, which places me in one of the most powerful age ranges of my society. I am upper-middle class, with an income sufficient to provide for myself and my family a lifestyle of comfort far above the majority who live in the United States and better than 98% of all people world-wide. I grew up in Birmingham, Alabama, in the United States of America, in the Deep South. The State in which I live has been one of the most racist, provincial, and segregated sub-societies in the U.S., and I have been profoundly affected by these attitudes of race and segregation. I am highly educated, with multiple networks of associations, in some of the most powerful circles of church and society in the city where I live. I am Protestant Clergy, in an established, well recognized religious denomination. I have traveled all over the world, and have multiple scholastic degrees, with honorary and merit certifications from multiple religious and civic organizations. I am heterosexual, married, with children. Because of these particularities, I occupy a position of power and privilege in my social context which places me in the uppermost percentage of access to influence, security, and opportunity. When I wear my clergy collar, I can walk into any setting and immediately have the respect and attention of anyone I choose.

I can never escape these particularities. These particularities will influence how I see the world, how I react to other persons, how I interpret my experience, and how I interpret my religious experience. However, other people from different social locations would interpret their experience of the very same cultural context very differently from how I interpret mine. In fact, other people, from very different social locations, would encounter and experience the world radically different from the way I do. Thus, the particularities of our "experience" define, expand, and/or limit our individual perspective on what we consider "real, right, or true."

Because our experience is an interpreted reality with multiple variables within multiple contexts, our experience, especially our religious experience, must be interpreted with great suspicion. A self-critical, multi-faceted interpretation will lay open our biases, assumptions, and values, so that we can see "with eyes wide open" our own cultural predispositions in order to understand more clearly how we approach and interpret our received religious tradition. One way of understanding how our experience is to be critiqued is to view experience, both individual and as a community of faith, as a "Sacred Text." Over the past century, multiple forms of interpretive hermeneutics have been developed to understand the Scriptures critically: Form Criticism, Redaction Criticism, Narrative Criticism, Cross-cultural Criticism, Liberationist Criticism, Feminist Criticism, Social-Scientific Criticism, and many others. All of these approaches take a specific point-of-view and offer analysis and interpretation of a Sacred Text so as to reveal historical, cultural particularities and offer a perspective on how the text, seen through a critical, interpretive lens, might be applied or understood in the context of our own time and situation. Our experience can and must be interpreted in similar ways. Just as we critically view a Sacred Text, we can view the particularities of our individual and/or communal perception, our "social location" and our historical trajectory. Our cultural bias embedded in our experience can then be brought to the surface and analyzed in the context of a thoughtful, prayerful discernment which will help us as faithful Christians be true to the Gospel of Jesus Christ, in the fullness of the gifts of the Holy Spirit.

Dr. Fernando Segovia, Professor of New Testament and Early Christianity at The Divinity School, Vanderbilt University, describes the profound impact of the newfound respect of "social location" and the consideration of the multiplicity of perspectives in the task of interpretation. In this excerpt, Dr. Segovia speaks of the impact upon Biblical studies of the awareness of "social location" and how this changes our view of a "sacred text." However, the same interpretive hermeneutic of "social location" applies to our own assumptions, perspectives, and interpretations of homosexual people:

> I see this irruption of the
> flesh-and-blood reader into biblical
> criticism as a harbinger not of
> anarchy and tribalism, as many
> who insist on impartiality and

objectivity often claim, but rather of continued de-colonization and liberation, of resistance and struggle against a subtle authoritarianism and covert tribalism of its own, in a discipline that has been, from beginning to end and top to bottom, thoroughly Eurocentric despite its assumed scientific persona of neutrality and universality. In effect, I regard the admission and intromission of real readers, of the contextuality and particularity of all readings, as an acceptance of the world for what it is, in the richness and fullness of its diversity, especially in this time of increasing and irreversible globalization in every sphere of life, including the theological and the interpretive—an acceptance of the "other" not as an imposed or defined "other" but as independent and self-defining. [94]

Another way of understanding the task of our interpretation of experience is in the language of H. Richard Neibuhr. Neibuhr describes this critical process of interpretation as a "time-full" interpretation.[95] Joseph Monti describes Neibuhr's perspective in this way:

> Biblical faith in general and Christian faith, made substantively material in the communities of Jesus Christ, are historical through and through. To be adequately faithful, the Church must continually engage in the struggle, as H. Richard Neibuhr suggests, to be "time-full" – to engage the past from the perspective of the present in terms of the future. If it has been the forgetfulness of the "time-full" dimensions of history and fidelity that has led the Church into its present circle of innervating anxiety about sexual morality, it will only be with a recovery of a full understanding of the historicity of Christian faith and life that we will break out. We must begin to self-consciously engage sexual ethics under the dual and dialectically equal obligations of fidelity and contemporaneity. Christian morality will certainly not affirm all that it finds in any given time and age, but if it is to be faithful, the Church must constructively engage its own contemporary worlds. Christianity is defined and identified as much

by its present as its past, cast
always upon the horizon of the
future. [96]

Our experience in dialogue and discernment in conversation with the experience of other people makes real our faith's truth-claims on our life. We trust our experience of the Holy Spirit in the life of the Church to move us forward in faith. The Holy Spirit illumines our understanding of God and creation, as well as the insights of the experiences of other people from a variety of points of view. The Holy Spirit motivates us to make sensitive moral judgments, not based just upon the experience of the majority or the point of view of those most privileged within the "Household of Faith," but also for those around us who's "social location" and experience the majority and the privileged within the faith do not understand or accept.

This diversity and conflict within human experience challenges our theological understanding. Yet, an awareness of a wider social reality brings to us serious theological reflection and shapes over and again the moral discernment of people of faith in the life of the church. Just as the Holy Spirit has moved the church throughout the past, just as we have heard the cries and moved toward the liberation of enslaved peoples, women, and other oppressed groups, the Holy Spirit is moving the church again to listen honestly to the experiences of homosexual people. This is the task of interpretation, always embedded in the discernment of our shared experience. When we open our hearts and share our experience, the Holy Spirit moves within and among us to make this experience an authority in our faith.

Edward Farley: Deep Symbols

One theologian who has made a great contribution to the understanding of interpretation/hermeneutics is Edward Farley, Professor of Theology at Vanderbilt Divinity School. In his book *Deep Symbols: Their Postmodern Effacement and Reclamation* [97], he has discussed the "Deep Symbols" which are embedded within our experience, which are the cultural assumptions carried by people, institutions, and societies, which define our perspective, under-gird our perception, and predict how we interpret the universe. Defining the Deep Symbols of our personal and social experience is an important interpretive hermeneutic in understanding how we see the world and understanding why persons and societies make the choices they do. What are Deep Symbols?

According to Farley, Deep Symbols are "Words of Power, that is, deep and enduring symbols that shape the values of a society and guide the life of faith, morality, and action." [98] Farley describes Deep Symbols as "values by which a community understands itself, from which it takes its aims, and to which it appeals as canons of cultural criticism. To grow up in a community is to have one's consciousness shaped by these symbols. Thus, they empower both individuals who live from them and the community that embodies them in narrative and ritual acts. They are Deep Symbols because they reside in perduring linguistic structures that maintain the community's very existence." [99]

To understand what Deep Symbols are, we can exclude what they are *not*. Deep Symbols are not specific acts or individual words or nouns that describe common actions within a culture. Deep Symbols are deeper than this. A Deep Symbol would convey a foundational concept, with expectations, values, and a "way of being in the world" for a society and individual more than a simple definition of a word or experience. For example, Farley uses Tradition, Law, and Obligation as examples of Deep Symbols in our culture. A Deep Symbol expresses assumptions, expectations, values, and relational consequences that are foundational to community and culture, in which there is a significant investment of persons and institutions at the most basic level, where something foundational within the culture is "at stake." Deep Symbols are connected: They are inter-related, intertwined with one another in a powerful support network of what Farley calls a "Master Narrative" of meaning, which, using the language of Peter Berger, constructs a "Sacred Canopy" of meaning, understanding, and perspective within a cultural world-view. [100]

Deep Symbols are not the "archetypes" of Carl Jung. For Jung, an archetype is a universal, cross-cultural, recurring image and pattern that exist in all of human interaction. Deep Symbols are instead more culturally dependent, having their impact within a finite time and space of understanding. Deep Symbols are "Words of Power" that are used, abused, applied, attacked, and manipulated by members of a specific society or community. These Deep Symbols are historical: They can rise and empower or they can lose their power and disappear over time. Deep Symbols are the primary motivating words of meaning in a society, relative to a particular community, and thus have the potential for change. Deep Symbols have at least the following four features: normativity, enchantment, fallibility, and location in a Master Narrative. [101] "In this respect, they are ideals that exercise a certain transcendence over a community and its members. This is why a community's prophets and visionaries can appeal to them to measure the community's corruption."[102] Deep Symbols have a motivating quality about them that can best be described as *enchanting*. Even in the midst of our secular society, people respond to these

Deep Symbols as if a "spell" has been cast upon them. Not, of course, in any magical way, but instead as a tool of motivation which will ellicit a passionate, devotional response. Words of power such as "rights," "democracy," "race," "freedom," and concepts such as "purity," "leadership," and "obligation" move people deeply to a response, for which many people in a society or community will even give their life. These Deep Symbols are thoroughly saturated and enmeshed in our cultural religious identity, yet are broader than any specific religious group. Deep Symbols hold together the entire culture, and are the center of meaning upon which the battle lines are drawn within competing groups and persons of power within a specific society.

One question that Farley explores which has enormous impact on the reality of Deep Symbols in our experience is that of the "postmodern" reality of our current culture. "Postmodern" is a word that attempts to describe the ambiguity and plurality of norms and values that cut across our shared cultural experience. As Farley describes it, postmodern is "a term for the historical shift, the rise of a new epoch, which names a liberation into plurality (from provincialisms), relativity (from absolutisms), and difference (from the old frozen authorities). At the same time it describes the void and anxiety we experience when our very selves are dispersed, bureaucratized, isolated, and rendered autonomous." [103] In the postmodern era, the Deep Symbols of traditional societies are on the defensive, vulnerable and attacked by the change, decay, and demise of firmly held assumptions within our culture. The question, for which we do not yet have an answer, is whether the change, decay, and demise of certain Deep Symbols within our society represents the general demise and destruction of our society and culture, or whether this change represents a positive transformation into a new and more healthy society. Is the postmodern era lost to decay into anomie and lawlessness? Or is the postmodern era a transitional moment in time where the constrictive power of specific Deep Symbols of the past/present are shed for a new birth of freedom and justice within redefined Deep Symbols that are more relevant and contemporary, which would restructure the Master Narrative of the culture at large? Is it decay or transformation? Perhaps it is both. Perhaps the answer to the question depends upon the social location of the person who answers it. As Farley says:

> One feature of Deep Symbols is their historical relativity, their necessary connection with specific people and cultures. Because they are relative, they are also vulnerable to change, decay, and even demise. To the degree that they function to maintain a people's communities, they are hard to kill. Nevertheless, they carry with them no guarantees of survival. The Deep Symbols of traditional societies were open to both transformation and historical demise. The merging of peoples, the ending of historical epochs, and the influence of new charismatic leaders ended some "words of power" and brought others into being. If a people are merged into the culture of another people, its Deep Symbols may disappear or survive in a new master narrative. What appears to be new in postmodern societies is not a

displacement of old symbols for new ones, but a weakening if not elimination of all "words of power." All Deep Symbols now appear to be imperiled by postmodern discourses, societal traits and sociologies of knowledge.[104]

Perhaps, if we step back and question a wider view, could the decay and/or transformation of Deep Symbols within our postmodern society be part of a transition of power relationships, representing a re-alignment of current world views and world dynamics? Could the destabilizing of long static Deep Symbols within our culture parallel a change from a Euro-dominated Western culture, where the destructive political history of Euro-colonialism and the dominance of nation states is being displaced by an economically and environmentally destructive multi-national corporatism and consumerism? Or could there be a movement in the opposite direction? At the same time, could the systems of traditional patriarchy be challenged by the emergence of Deep Symbols associated with a "merit society," less dominated by the Deep Symbols related to sexism and homophobia? These and many other parallel and related trajectories can be proposed in the current uncertainties related to the "shaking of the foundations" now taking place.

Whatever the case, Farley continues to affirm the reality and power of Deep Symbols in postmodern societies. "There are reasons to resist the notion that postmodern societies are utterly bereft of Deep Symbols. Deep Symbols do continue to empower the language of at least some communities and some movements of cultural criticism. Appeals to such symbols continue to be made in the public sphere, and these appeals are not without their power." [105]

As we interpret our experience as individuals, as a community of faith, and as a culture, we must be aware of the place and power of Deep Symbols. These Deep Symbols reflect what is most important with a society and culture. These Deep Symbols -- how they have developed, how they have been challenged, and how they have changed over time -- offer us a way of understanding how we as individuals and communities of faith have been formed and motivated, both in the struggles around their defense, and in the struggles we have witnessed in their transformation. To understand the trajectories of Deep Symbols over time is to interpret the environment we currently experience in the "culture wars" of our contemporary church and society.

Deep Symbol: Marriage

In the context of this discussion, what are the Deep Symbols of our culture related to the great conflict in church and society about the place, status and acceptance of homosexual persons? What might these Deep Symbols be? Certainly, there are Deep Symbols related to sexuality that impact how homosexual persons are perceived and treated in church and society. However, I would suggest that the dominant Deep Symbol related to the current "culture war" over gay and lesbian persons would be the Deep Symbol of "marriage."

Marriage is one of the most hotly debated issues/symbols on the social/political landscape of 21st century America. In Connecticut, on Oct. 10, 2008, the State Supreme Court said that "separate is not equal," and it is unconstitutional to discriminate against gay men and lesbians in marriage. The 85-page decision written by Justice Richard N. Palmer said the State Legislature singled out gay men and lesbians for differential treatment by creating a separate legal classification for gays who, like married couples, wish to have their relationships recognized under law with civil unions in 2005. "Ultimately the message is that what same-sex couples have is not as important or as significant as "real marriage," the decision reads. Thus, Connecticut joins Massachusetts in legalizing gay marriage. The decision goes on to say: "We conclude that, in light of the history of pernicious discrimination faced by gay men and lesbians, and because the institution of marriage carries with it a status and significance that the newly created classification of civil unions does not embody, the segregation of heterosexual and homosexual couples into separate institutions constitutes a cognizable harm" [106]

In the November elections of 2008, the State of California voted to ban gay marriage by a surprisingly large margin, reversing the State Supreme Court decision legalizing gay marriage in 2007. Of course, proponents of gay marriage immediately challenged the results of the election in the California Supreme Court. Across the country, electoral bans on gay marriage were approved in eight different states. Surprisingly, on the same day that Barak Obama, a liberal African-American Democrat, was elected President of the United States, gay marriage was universally voted down in every state where it appeared on the ballot. It is interesting to me that, in California, the demographic group most responsible for "tipping the scale" toward a ban on gay marriage were the Mormons (The Church of Jesus Christ of Latter Day Saints), the Christian denomination most commonly associated with the practice of polygamy. Why would this Christian denomination so fundamentally patriarchal, so historically abusive to the rights of women, be so passionately opposed to gay rights? Perhaps there is an association between the two? [107]

In churches and Christian denominations across the country, the issue of same-sex marriage is passionately debated. This issue is at the core of the potential split of the Anglican Communion world-wide. In the Episcopal Church of the United States, as well as other churches in Communion with the Church of England, Bishops and Dioceses are divided about the role and place of gay marriage within the church. In the United Methodist Church, debate is passionate and heated. The United Methodist Church in the United States is regionally split, with most Methodists in the North and West in favor of gay marriage; while most Methodists in the South are firmly against it.

Why is the marriage of two people of the same sex so hotly debated and so passionately conflicted in our society? Why are some people so angry and offended at the very idea of same-sex marriage? The answer seems to lie within the deeply held beliefs and assumptions of the majority of the people in American culture. These beliefs and assumptions may or may not be critically examined, but they are deeply felt. My experience is that this issue impacts the individual and society at the most foundational, emotional level, because marriage is one of the central Deep Symbols of our culture and society.

Marriage is a Deep Symbol because it is, as Farley defines it, a deep and enduring symbol that shapes and guides the life, faith, morality and action of our society. Marriage is a Deep Symbol in that it defines the consciousness of expectations and understandings we have for ourselves and the people of our society, and it empowers individuals through the narratives that define us and the ritual acts that affirm our collective experience. Whether in full affirmation of its meaning, or in radical rejection of its expectations, the Deep Symbol of marriage is a foundational "Word of Power" that is used, abused, applied, attacked, and manipulated by members of our society to influence, interpret, and define each other.

Marriage, as a Deep Symbol, has a "normative" quality in that it sets a cultural mark of definition on a person. To be "married" carries with it cultural baggage that defines the individual. Even in the diversity of 21st century America, to not be within the cultural confines of traditional marriage is to be outside the norm. Marriage certainly has the quality of "enchantment." Marriage is for many an "ideal" that has a "transcendent" impact upon the members of our society. All one has to do is attend just one wedding to appreciate the "spell" of the cultural impact that takes place upon a couple who go through an almost magical transformation in the eyes of a community in the midst of a wedding ritual. Of course, the ritual of a wedding is not magical as in a fantasy world; however, the motivation, passion, and devotion given to the ritual of a wedding by those who participate in it, and those who witness it, make the event of entering into marriage a truly "enchanting" experience. The deep impact of marriage, in multiple ways, especially in the "enchantment" that surrounds it, clearly defines it as a Deep Symbol in our culture, by which communities have been formed, boundaries established, over which battle lines have been drawn, and passionate conflicts arise.

Farley also describes Deep Symbols as having the characteristic of "fallibility." It is this "fallibility" that sets the stage for conflict. The term fallibility describes Deep Symbols as having an inherently relative, time-specific, culturally determined rise and fall within a society. Members of a society are often not aware of the cultural relativity of their shared Deep Symbols. And they typically defend these Deep Symbols, such as marriage, as if they are, and always have been, a constant throughout time. In our postmodern era, the Deep Symbol of marriage is on the defensive, vulnerable and attacked by the change, decay, and demise of firmly held assumptions about this institution within our culture. Thus, leaders, who compete for power and authority within society, employ and manipulate the Deep Symbol of marriage to suit their particular ends.

It is not just in postmodern societies that marriage has undergone dramatic changes as a "fallible" Deep Symbol. Marriage, like other Deep

Symbols, has always been in flux, always in the midst of change. As Professor Mary Ann Tolbert has already told us: "Marriage is not, as some commentators, politicians, and even religious leaders, have recently contended, an "unchanging tradition of thousands of years." Rather, marriage, like all other social institutions is quite variable and has gone through many different forms over the course of history and across many cultures." [108] Yet, this "fallibility" and variation within the Deep Symbol of marriage is one of the central issues around which the "culture war" in our society is raging. Traditionalists and conservatives in the religious and social arenas of our society are in vigorous defense of the Deep Symbol of marriage, traditionally and legally defined as a man and a woman, defending it with appeals to the Bible, cultural assumptions, and long codified legal standards.

And so, the question remains as to the meaning and message of the Deep Symbol of marriage and its place within the "Master Narrative" of our 21st century society. As Farley makes us ask:

Could the decay and/or transformation of Deep Symbols within our postmodern society be part of a transition of power relationships, representing a re-alignment of current world-views and world-dynamics? It seems to me that the transformation and transition of the Deep Symbol of marriage is a necessary step in the right direction towards justice and equality for all people. Instead of defining marriage from only the point of view of the dominant, heterosexual majority, we could transform it and define marriage as a human right, where two people could formalize their committed, monogamous, life-long relationship on the basis cited above in the Connecticut Supreme Court decision: No longer separate and unequal, but guaranteeing universal and equal access to civil rights to all people under the law. As the church, we can offer the recognition of same-sex marriage based on a moral commitment to equality and justice for all people, and a belief that "human sexual orientations, whether heterosexual or homosexual, are a gift from God", as affirmed by The United Church of Canada's 37th General Council.[109]

Why do we need to struggle for this change in the institution of marriage? Why battle the powers and principalities of American culture? Why struggle to transform this Deep Symbol of marriage so that it will be inclusive for *all* people? Why? Because marriage matters deeply in how people are treated, in how they live their lives in a nation that claims to be a "just" society. The marriage relationship as a Deep Symbol in our culture is central to how a person is culturally, socially, religiously perceived and treated in society. Marriage is recognized in law, protecting both parties with rights and privileges and ensuring the protection and care of any children in the family. For example: Married partners can adopt each other's children; in the case of divorce they have legal rights that govern fair property settlement, spousal or child support, access to children, and the right to remain in the family home; they can sponsor their partner as an immigrant; and they are protected by conflict of interest laws. The marriage relationship is recognized in times of illness or death. A common-law or married spouse is considered the closest next of kin and has the right to make decisions about medical or personal care, about funerals or burial. Married couples automatically also have financial rights and benefits, such as the right to be included on a company benefits plan, spousal income tax deductions, and the right to inherit the estate of the deceased partner or to receive pension or survival benefits.

Shall the church stand for justice for *all* people or not? Shall the church treat people fairly and demand the state to do the same? Shall the church be a fortress for the sake of the majority, blindly opposing people in the minority whom it does not understand? Or, shall the church be led by the Holy Spirit to defend the rights of all people? Shall the church narrowly define who is worthy of equality and justice and exclude the sexual minority? Or, shall the church be led by the Holy Spirit and affirm that all our children, gay and straight, are worthy of an equal place in church and society? Shall the church define as unclean or "incompatible" some of our children and abandon them?

Just as the Holy Spirit has moved the church throughout the past to challenge the Deep Symbols that harm people and societies, just as we have heard the cries, and moved toward the liberation of enslaved peoples, women, and other oppressed groups, the Holy Spirit is moving the church again to listen honestly to the experiences of homosexual people. The Holy Spirit is moving the church again. This is the task of interpretation and discernment, always embedded in our experience.

Chapter Five:
Word and Sacrament:
Prophetic Nonviolence and Radical Hospitality

Mary is the oldest of four children. As a child she was a natural leader with the gift of gab: Mary could talk about anything. As a little girl, she had a wonderful and active sense of humor. She was always laughing and joking around. While growing up she was often called a "tom-boy" because she could play baseball as well as the guys. However, it was not the guys that she preferred. Mary knew from early on that she wanted to be around other girls, not boys. Mary grew up as an active member in the United Methodist Church. When High School came around, Mary went through the usual drill of dates and proms; however, this was a role she was playing, not who she knew herself to be. Mary never told her parents about her budding sexual orientation. She was very private about what she felt about other young women. Even in college, Mary did not stray from the expected heterosexual routine she dutifully performed. Though she would politely participate in the expected interaction of dating men, she never had relationships that lasted very long. Instead, it was her friendship with other women that gave her the most meaning and satisfaction. It was the intimacy, the deep companionship, and the fulfillment that these relationships brought which drew her closer and closer to women, and farther away from men. Mary graduated with a degree in Education. She decided she would also get her

*Masters in Education. In her first course in the
Masters program, she met the love of her life. Cindy
was also in the Masters program, and they quickly
became fast friends. Cindy was a lesbian. She had
earlier come to know her sexual orientation, and she
had explored her sexuality before. Cindy was
confident in who she was as a lesbian. As Cindy and
Mary's relationship became deeper, Cindy was able
to invite Mary into a lesbian relationship that was
the most natural, fulfilling, and blissful union that
Mary could imagine. Mary and Cindy have been
together for many years, in a faithful, monogamous
loving relationship, which the State and the church
refuse to acknowledge or bless. Neither Mary nor
Cindy want anything to do with the United Methodist
Church. In the religious institution where she was
baptized, Mary feels totally unwelcomed.*

Where do we go from here? How can we
incorporate a reading of Scripture that does not seek
to use it as a weapon of exclusion? How can we
view Tradition as a critical tool of analysis that
shows us our mistakes and guides us to more faithful
discipleship? How can we view science and its
evidence as a reasonable discourse where we can
discern together what is true? How can we open our
hearts to the Experience of the Holy Spirit by those

people who are different from us? As we reflect back upon the arguments above, we must ask, "What does this mean for the church and its ministry?" Where must the church lead when confronted by the arguments calling us to repent from our exclusion of gay and lesbian people? Where must the church lead in order to shape a theology and ministry that fully welcomes gay and lesbian people? We must open our hearts to one another in the way of Jesus.

Prophetic Nonviolence

The first step the church must take is a rigorous and humbling confession of our addiction to violence. By violence I mean not just physical violence, but emotional, relational, spiritual, and institutional violence as well. We must confront the ways we participate in violence. We must confess our violence toward gay and lesbian people, and our addiction to violence in general. In my opinion, all forms of violence are deeply connected to each other. As we have read the stories of individuals who have been abused by the church, and explore an honest assessment of the history of the church, we must first confess how violence and its destructive effect exists in our own hearts, and how it corrupts the behavior of our religious institutions.

The Christian church, since early in its history, has been seduced and has succumbed to the temptation of the "Powers and Principalities" of this world, and has embraced violence as a necessity. This reality has been confirmed and documented by many, many writers, who clearly demonstrate this through historical research. Although lengthy books have been written which demonstrate this reality, a short review of the church's early descent into paths of violence is needed.

Jesus of Nazareth began a radical movement of nonviolence that challenged the religious, social, and political values of his day. Jesus called forth a group of men and women who held all things in common, practiced baptism as an initiation rite, and participated in a common meal where all people were welcomed. The followers of Jesus sought the "Kingdom of God" ("Reign of God" or "Empire of God,"), where justice, righteousness, forgiveness, nonviolence, and a commitment to the poor and marginalized were central values; over and against the Roman Empire where violence, domination, occupation, and oppression were central values. The "Kingdom of God" commitments and values taught by Jesus were lived out both in the "here and now," as well as at the expectation of the "end of the age," when the fullness of the kingdom would come. The Jesus Community lived a radical ethic of nonviolence, even loving their enemy. They welcomed the stranger and the outcast into their group. The Jesus Community typically came from the poor, and showed great concern for the poor. They taught that the heart of the Law is to love your neighbor as you love yourself. They taught that God is love; and that we are to forgive others as God has forgiven us. The Torah and the Prophets were embraced as the Word of God by the Jesus Movement; however, the central emphasis in their interpretation of the Hebrew Bible was placed upon passages which lifted up compassion, love, justice, nonviolence, and forgiveness. All of these assumptions about the Jesus Movement and its community are grounded in a faithful reading of the

New Testament, and in the witness of multiple academic sources by scholars such as Borg, Crossan, Patterson, Wink, Tolbert, Segovia, and many, many others.

As the Jesus Movement became the church, over the course of three centuries it was greatly persecuted and abused by the violence of the Roman Empire. Eventually, the church grew to the point that it threatened the previously dominant Roman Imperial Cult of paganism. Remarkably, the church became the dominant religious expression within the Roman Empire of late antiquity. Emperor Constantine, in the early 4th century, declared Christianity as the official state religion of the Roman Empire. However, as the church moved through time, it began to conform itself to the values of the "Powers and Principalities" of the world rather than being fully faithful to the teachings of Jesus. The interests of the church became closely aligned with the interests of Imperial Rome. Purges and political violence became synonymous with church politics, and the church, once persecuted, became the persecutor. [110]

Then the church turned not only against the "unbeliever" but also turned on its own, labeling and persecuting those who might disagree with "orthodoxy" as "heretics." One only has to take a quick look at church history to see that it is filled with the suffering and blood of those who did not fit into the mold set by those who claimed to lead the church. Often, sincere believers participated in heinous acts of violence in order to "save the church" from the influence of dissenters. At other times, opportunistic people took advantage of the fears of others in order to increase their own wealth and power. The official sanction of state violence and the blessing of violence by ecclesiastical authorities have brought about hundreds of years of torture and persecution. Officially sanctioned persecution and violence has taken the form of the torture and death of those who presented ideas or theologies outside "orthodoxy," crusades and wars, Inquisitions and witch-hunts, ethnic cleansings, slavery, and Jim Crow segregation.[111] This violence is not just limited to physical violence. Emotional and spiritual violence has crippled the witness of the church. Emotional harassment and spiritual condemnation await those who dare to be outside the norm.

Since the days of Emperor Constantine, the church has embraced violence as a necessity, with devastating consequences. The church has embraced the values of "Empire," defending the violence of the State, and diluting the prophetic call of Jesus to nonviolence to the point of silence. In our own time, the church's relationship with violence is documented by Walter Wink in his book, *The Powers That Be: Theology for a New Millennium.* [112] He describes the church and society's acceptance and commitment toward violence as the illusion of "Redemptive Violence." [113] We have been seduced into believing that violence against others will protect us, even save us. All the while, the destructive consequences of violence continue to destroy us. Our collective commitment to violence exists in our common spirituality that affects every concentric circle of our life: Our understanding of God, our relationship with self, our relationship and behavior in the family, and our social institutions of church and government.

We are saturated with an ideology of violence. We see it in the cultural expressions and behaviors around us: The television is saturated with violence. Movies, even cartoons for children, are saturated with violence. As a culture, the United States is saturated with violent crime, including violence against women and the abuse of children in numbers greater than what is found in other so called "developed" countries.[114] We continue to execute prisoners in the United States, with many church leaders endorsing this last act of violence as appropriate punishment in the name of God.

For the church, as has been thoroughly discussed in Chapter 2 in our examination of the theology of atonement, our understanding of God and the behavior of God in our own experience is powerfully distorted by our collective assumptions of the importance and value of violence in our history and our everyday life. This theology of violence powerfully impacts everything about our life. Our own self understanding, and our identity formed in the context of our family is deeply affected by violence: Domestic physical violence has been uncovered as a consistent and toxic presence in our lives. Beyond physical violence, emotional abuse of children and spouses can only be described as epidemic in proportion. [115]

The result of our cultural and religious commitment to "Redemptive Violence" means that the toxic influence of violence surrounds us and influences us at every level. The influence reveals itself in our patterns of behavior in our social and political action. The "preemptive strike" policies of our government in the war in Iraq, and the collective endorsement of this violence by the majority of Americans (and Christians in America) when the war began are painful and horrific examples of what our church's passive or active endorsement of violence can produce. The impact of violence runs deep. John Bradshaw describes the impact of our culture of violence as producing what he calls "The Sickness of the Soul: Shame." [116] Violence and its poisonous pedagogy is "the source of most of the disturbing inner states that deny full human life.

Depression, alienation, self-doubt, isolating loneliness, paranoid and schizoid phenomena, compulsive disorders, splitting of the self, perfectionism, a deep sense of inferiority, inadequacy or failure, the so-called borderline conditions and disorders of narcissism—all result from shame" brought on by violence. [117]

The results of violence, and our culture of violence, both within and around the church, have had a lethal impact on gay and lesbian people. In the stories that have been shared in this book, as well as many, many others that I have heard told by those who have suffered, is evidence that the level of violence (physical, emotional, spiritual, and institutional) endured by homosexual people cannot be underestimated. In their book, *We Were Baptized, Too*, Marilyn Alexander and James Preston, a lesbian woman and gay man, relate the spiritual violence they have experienced:

> Gays and lesbians are silenced by
> the hatred and fear of the society in
> which we live, the fears of the
> families into which they were born,
> and the institutionalized prejudice

of the Church, which at one time pledged to nurture and support. Gay and lesbian people are also silenced by their own self-hatred, fear and prejudice. Gay and lesbian Christians are silenced by homophobia. Writer and activist Suzanne Pharr defines "homophobia" as "the irrational fear and hatred of those who love and sexually desire those of the same sex." This fear and hatred are what very often seal the lips of lesbian and gay Christians. They know the possible results of ending the silence. They know that to "come out" may mean rejection by friends, loss of employment, threats against their life, and banishment from their families. They can see the possibilities of losing children, being beaten or bashed, suffering rape, losing life – losing everything. Homophobia does an excellent job of silencing gays/lesbians, and it also keeps non-gays and non-lesbians trapped, unable to move beyond their own fears. It is this life of silence that is continually reinforced and undergirded by the Church, and it is this life of silence that brings so much pain. [118]

My own experience as a pastor in the United Methodist Church confirms their experience. Over the past 20 years, in every church that I have served, gay and lesbian people, their parents, and friends have been present. In every instance, there has been a universal understanding and expectation that **no one** is to speak about homosexuality, their experience as gay and lesbian people, or their spirituality as gay persons. The only way homosexual persons can exist in the church has been to be silent.

This spiritual violence of silence and the spiritual violence of institutional rejection bring deadly consequences. Although it is not necessarily the "church" that is participating in the physical violence done to gay and lesbian people, the spiritual violence of rejection and condemnation by the church lends itself to the encouragement of physical violence by others in society. The following stories are from Robert Buchanan's book *Love, Honor, and Respect: How to Confront Homosexual Bias and Violence in Christian Culture*, which demonstrate the horrific results of the chain of violence in which the spiritual violence of the church is a passive participant:

> Private Calvin Glover bludgeoned Private First Class Barry Winchell to death with a baseball bat at Fort Campbell, Kentucky. Winchell had been harassed and threatened at the Army base. His platoon was known to chant the cadence: "Faggot faggot, down the street, shoot him shoot him, 'till he retreats."
>
> Arthur was savagely kicked and beaten to death and then run over by a car. He had told his support group at a nearby college of threats, name calling, and having things thrown at him in the small Appalachian town where he lived. Arthur had been "outed" as gay.
>
> Roberto was walking home alone through his apartment complex in Phoenix. Reportedly, he was minding his own business when he was confronted by a group of four teenagers. One of the teenagers took out a handgun and shot him in the chest, ending his life. Roberto was 36 years old.

Police arrested a suspect and connected the young man to another murder the previous year of a 71 year old man. The reason that police gave for both of the murders is that the teens knew both men to be gay. The same group was responsible for graffiti, threats, and property damage throughout the city at establishments where gay and lesbian people gathered.

Brian, a 45 year old resident of San Francisco, had just left a bar frequented by gay men. On the street, he was accosted by a man apparently intoxicated, yelling hate slogans and epithets at him. He was beaten and fell to the ground. He became unconscious after hitting his head on the pavement. Brian died from his injuries.

Andrew's strangled body was found naked in the woods near his Newport News, Virginia home. The man who was convicted of Andrew's murder was also convicted in eleven other cases in the Tidewater area of Virginia. Andrew is believed to be the last of the twelve victims of the serial killer. All of his victims were gay, and were killed because they were gay.

Matthew, a 21 year old college student, was deceived into leaving a bar with two friends. He was taken outside Laramie, Wyoming, where he was brutally beaten, and his body left hanging on a fence in inhumane temperatures. He died from his injuries. The reason for the attack was reported to be that Matthew had been open about his homosexuality: He simply admitted being gay to his assailants. To add insult to this atrocious act, an organization from a nearby university included the mocking image of a scarecrow on its homecoming float a few days later in their Homecoming Parade, publicly referencing and laughing at this horrible incident, which later became more widely known as a national news story. [119]

Other homosexual people have been chased by vehicles, harassed at work, and discriminated against in every imaginable way, simply for being homosexual. These are only a few examples of the many Hate Crimes documented each year by the Southern Poverty Law Center in Montgomery, Alabama. [120]

The first thing the church must do is to confess our participation, encouragement, or endorsement of any forms of violence of thought, word, or deed toward homosexual people. With God's help, we must break through our collective denial of our violence toward gay and lesbian people. Only after we repent of our physical, emotional, spiritual, and institutional violence and seek to change the culture within and around the church will we have the capacity to begin the healing from our exclusion and abuse of gay and lesbian people. Then we will be following Jesus in our relationship with gay and lesbian people.

Next, the church must welcome gay and lesbian people into the fullness of the relationship they deserve in the community of faith, and make a faithful commitment to a prophetic, nonviolent activism on behalf of homosexual people. It is not enough to repent. The church must not be afraid to speak loudly and act decisively for an end to the physical, emotional, spiritual, and institutional violence against homosexual people, and enter into the fray of political decision making on the local and national level. Laws, as well as hearts and minds, need to be changed. Walter Wink, in his book *Jesus and Nonviolence: The Third Way*, describes this dynamic:

> Most Christians desire nonviolence, yes, but they are not talking about a nonviolent struggle for justice. They mean simply the absence of conflict. They would like the system to change without having to be involved in changing it. What they mean by nonviolence is as far from Jesus' "third way" as a lazy nap in the sun is from confrontation in which protesters are being clubbed to the ground. When a church that has not lived out a costly identification with the oppressed offers to mediate between hostile parties, it merely adds to the total impression that it wants to stay above the conflict and not take sides. The church says to the lion and lamb, "Here, let me negotiate a truce," to which the lion

replies, "Fine, after I finish my lunch. [121]

As Gandhi said, "You must be the change you seek in this world." The church must repent of its homophobia, then *be* the change it desires in seeking nonviolent transformation in the institutions that surround us.

When we as Christians embrace the truth that Jesus was and is the nonviolent Prince of Peace, and make a commitment to living nonviolently in every area of our life, a transformation will happen. We will begin to interpret the authorities of Christianity with greater faithfulness to Jesus. We will begin to read Scripture differently. When viewing the text through the nonviolent eyes of Jesus, we will be more Christ-like in our interpretation, rejecting any response that leads to violence. We will begin to view the Tradition of the church differently. Instead of viewing the past through the dogmatic lens of a ridged orthodoxy, we will see Tradition through the corrective lens of the nonviolent peace of Jesus. In doing this, the failures of the church will become more clearly visible, and the true saints of the church will be lifted up. We will begin to embrace the reason and diligence of scientific research with greater humility and attentiveness. Instead of arrogantly battling the scientific community for superiority, we can embrace science as a partner in the search for greater knowledge, clarity, and understanding. Embracing all truth as God's truth will lead us by faith to a greater unity in seeking peace and justice for all people. And, our experience of the Holy Spirit will greatly increase in the life of the church when we put aside our fear, suspicion, and hatred of those people who are different from ourselves, and make a commitment to nonviolent, peaceful relationships, even with our enemies. All of this would have a profound impact upon how the church relates to gay and lesbian people, and how the different sides of the conflict over homosexuality in the church might come to a faithful resolution.

In Dr. Martin Luther King's last address to the Southern Christian Leadership Conference, he made a passionate plea for the leaders of church and society to embrace the way of nonviolence:

This is the time for action. What is needed is a strategy for change, a tactical program that will bring change to the mainstream of American life as quickly as possible. So far, this has only been offered by the nonviolent movement. Without recognizing this we will end up with solutions that don't solve, answers that don't answer, and explanations that don't explain. And I say to you today, that I still stand by nonviolence. And I am still convinced that it is the most potent weapon available in the struggle for justice in this country. And the other thing is that I am concerned about a better world. I'm concerned about justice. I'm concerned about brotherhood. I'm concerned about truth. And when one is concerned about these, one can never advocate violence. For through violence you may murder the murderer but you can't murder murder. Through violence you may murder a liar but you can't establish truth. Through violence you may murder the hater, but you can't murder hate. Darkness cannot put out darkness. Only light can do that. And I say to you, I have also decided to stick to love. For I know that love is

ultimately the only answer to our
problems. And I'm going to talk
about it everywhere I go. I know it
isn't popular to talk about love in
some circles today. I'm not talking
about emotional bosh when I talk
about love. I'm talking about a
strong, demanding love; because
I've seen too much hate. [122]

A Prophetic Ministry of Active Nonviolence

It is not enough to have a "correct" opinion
about the nonviolence of Jesus. It is not enough to
sit on the sidelines and critique and complain about
the violence of the church and society. There must
be a prophetic ministry of active nonviolence that is
inclusive of *all* people. The church must self-
critically embody and teach the nonviolent way of
Jesus Christ. I am blessed to have the opportunity to
lead a prophetic ministry of active nonviolence
where I serve at Church of the Reconciler in
Birmingham, Alabama. In this chapter, I will
describe the context of my ministry and offer a
program of ministry that conforms itself to a

Christian theology of nonviolence and radical hospitality for an inclusive ministry to gay and lesbian people.

A House of Prayer For All People

In 1992, in Birmingham, Alabama, six United Methodist Churches closed. The buildings were sold, and the ministry of the church in the city was profoundly wounded. Of these six churches, two of them at one time were numbered among the largest Methodist Churches in the State of Alabama. Over the course of the past 40 years, these churches had declined and closed because of racism. The pastor of one of these churches, the Rev. Lawton Higgs, Sr., had desperately tried to turn one of these churches outward toward ministry to its community and had failed. The McCoy United Methodist Church could not overcome the "genetic imprint" of its Klan-based theology of racial segregation. Although it had been decades since the Ku Klux Klan infested "Citizens Council" meetings had been held in the basement of the church, whose members conspired in the bombings against those who were involved in the Civil Rights Movement. [123] Although it had been decades since the most rabid racist members had moved out of the community in the "white flight" of the 1960's and 1970's, the collective consciousness of the congregation could not move beyond the ingrained concept that their church was for "Whites Only."

In response to the closing of these churches, Rev. Higgs asked to be appointed to a new church start in downtown Birmingham that would be intentionally multi-cultural and interracial, so that the United Methodist Church would make a witness against the racism of its past and present, and make a commitment to being in ministry in the city. This proposal was greeted with serious opposition by powerful staff members of the North Alabama Conference of the United Methodist Church. One staff member said that "Blacks and Whites would never worship together in Birmingham" and "This would be a waste of money." However, Bishop

Robert Fannin, recognizing the serious need in the city, agreed to begin the new church.

For 18 months, the core group of the new church start began attending churches of every racial background in the metro area of Birmingham. This racially integrated group found that Sunday morning was the most segregated time of the week. They put together a plan to invite people of all races, ethnic groups, and nationalities to their first worship service on May 22nd, 1994. After gathering this unlikely band of believers together, they meet every Sunday in a store-front in downtown Birmingham. They embraced the city center with a commitment to open the door for all people as a "House of Prayer for All People." The new church was indeed multi-cultural and interracial; however, the new members of the new church were predominantly well-educated and middle-class.

To the shock of the pastor and new members of the church, what greeted them when they opened the door wide was a flood of homeless and destitute people. Although the pastor and church members were very sophisticated and learned on the realities of issues related to race, they were completely unaware of the massive numbers of homeless and destitute people who lived on the streets of downtown Birmingham, and were spiritually challenged in trying to deal with the magnitude of the problem.

Quickly the new church, now named Church of the Reconciler, faced a serious crisis: Would they be "A House of Prayer for All People" – except for the homeless and destitute? Or, would they truly be a "House of Prayer for All People"? Many of the members who were attracted to the original vision of the congregation could not bear the constant interruption and desperate pleading of the homeless. Almost all of the staff and members of the church were caught up in a relationship to the homeless borne out of the stigma and stereotypes that had been culturally ingrained in them about homeless people. They did not know who the homeless were, how these destitute people became homeless, or how to be in ministry with them.

The presence of the homeless was overwhelming. These desperate homeless people interrupted worship services and harassed people for money or other forms of aide. They smelled terrible. They were sick or crippled. They were mentally ill. They provided a constant stream of confrontation and stress that threatened to wear down even the most patient and conscientious believer. Some of the members left the church in frustration.

However, the church studied the scriptures, and struggled in prayerful discernment about how to deal with this burden. By the work of the Holy Spirit, they chose to follow Jesus and welcome the outcast and the poor into the fellowship of the congregation. Though it was very difficult, Church of the Reconciler refused to turn anyone away, and began a theological and ministerial shift: Adding to the focus on racial justice and reconciliation, they accepted the commitment to seek justice and reconciliation with and for the homeless poor. The irony is that in giving themselves to a ministry by and with the homeless poor, Church of the Reconciler became more fully multi-cultural and interracial. The homeless poor come from practically every racial, economic, educational, and religious class or group in the world. In the prophetic announcement of Isaiah 55:8, we hear that "my thoughts are not your thoughts, nor are your ways my ways, says the LORD." (NRSV) By God's grace, Church of the Reconciler has become what it hoped to be, but by a very different road than had been anticipated.

The most basic need of the homeless in Birmingham that the church could meet was food, so Church of the Reconciler began offering a meal whenever it opened. Soon the numbers of hungry homeless became more than the church could handle alone. The church realized that they could not respond to the ministry need at their door without help. The church began begging the larger, wealthier congregations in the city for help, by God's grace, these churches responded. At first it was the support from the United Methodist Women, providing money for the church to purchase food and offer other ministries. If not for the early support of the UMW, Church of the Reconciler would have never survived. The next most needed ministry was a Clothes Closet. Without a place to bathe or wash clothes, a change of clothes is always needed. Once again, the church appealed to other congregations for support. A Clothes Closet began so that homeless men, women, and children would have clothes to wear.

However, Church of the Reconciler was about more than just handing out meals and clothes. The church made a holistic and determined commitment to study, pray, worship, and serve *with* the poor *as* the church. The homeless were enthusiastically invited to become members and participate fully in the life of the congregation.

As the years have progressed, the ministry at Church of the Reconciler has grown exponentially. The church has moved to a much larger facility. The church is now located in old warehouse in inner city Birmingham that has been converted into a church. In January of 2006, I was appointed pastor at Church of the Reconciler, to work with my father, Lawton Higgs, Sr., who in his "retirement" continues to work full time in ministry at the church. An Assistant Pastor has been added to our staff, as well as several lay volunteer staff members. We average over 150 people in each of our worship services. Each day, over 300 homeless men, women, and children come into our church and are served a meal, offered clothing, and are served by our staff and volunteers, who assist them in finding housing, jobs, transportation, medical care, social services, veterans services, recovery from addiction, and legal aid. We have a Community Service program where homeless people can "work off" their fines and warrants instead of serving time in jail. We have a jail ministry that serves the Birmingham City Jail and the Jefferson County Jail. We have a Children's Program, offering Sunday School and After School Enrichment. In 2008, we served over 1500 plates of food each week. Each one of these meals is served by another congregation in the Birmingham Area, called by the Holy Spirit to share the food they have with the poor. In 2008, over 3000 volunteers from all across the country, from diverse ecumenical and multi-faith backgrounds, have come to serve food, stock the clothes closet, shepherd the children, and assist in worship, education, and discipleship. These volunteers are not present at Church of the

Reconciler to "hand down" or "hand out" resources to the homeless. Every encounter between the middle class and the homeless is structured so that all the people, from every different background, work together as equals in the task of serving the church in the peace of Christ. For example, the churches who bring the food for our daily meal work side by side in the kitchen with the homeless members of Church of the Reconciler. In working this way, we break down barriers of division, and build friendships and understanding by the power of the Spirit. We are not about "charity." We are about building a community of justice and peace in the name of Jesus Christ.

Studying the Scriptures, reading the witnesses of the saints, working in communion with the homeless poor, in the context of ministry on the street in the brutality of the urban Birmingham landscape, we at Church of the Reconciler have been changed in how we understand the Christian faith. We began to see who has power, and who is powerless. We began to hear the voices and see the needs of those whom we had not previously heard.

We began to see how the values, assumptions, and structures of "Empire" are powerfully present in church and society in the oppression of the poor. Through their eyes, we see how the homeless poor are unwelcome in most churches in the metro area. And, from our fellowship with African-American Christians, we learn from them that they are still unwelcome in most White churches in Birmingham. We hear over and again how the poor are oppressed by the structural, institutional systems that keep them in poverty: There is not a "living wage" for the poor. A homeless person can work 40 hours a week at the current typical wage, and not make enough money to pay rent, utilities, transportation, and housing. Thus, once a person becomes homeless, he/she is caught in a vicious, violent cycle that keeps that person homeless. There is very little medical care available for the homeless. Emergency rooms might bandage their cuts and wounds, but rarely admit them into the hospital, and always send them out with prescriptions for medication that they cannot afford. Police harassment and brutality are a constant presence for the homeless community. The homeless poor are constantly being harassed and arrested for the smallest of crimes, often for just urinating in public when they have no restroom facilities open to them. I have personally witnessed on numerous occasions the Birmingham Police taze and beat mentally ill homeless men who did not follow their directions quickly enough. All of the above is institutionalized violence against the poor. All of these are witnesses that the values and violence of "Empire" are firmly operative in our society: violent abuse of the poor. The homeless and working poor live a life no better than slaves, and are run into the ground by a callous dysfunctional political/social/economic system.

In the crucible that is Church of the Reconciler, a new theology of Radical Hospitality that expresses a new vision for the church and the city has been refined by the members of the church. Our theology has its **primary** root in the ministry of Jesus, as he welcomed the outcast and the sinner as beloved before God and practiced "open commensality" at the table. Jesus challenged the violence of a religious purity system, and the violence of Empire with the nonviolent Reign of God; so do we. Our theology at Church of the Reconciler has its roots in the Apostle Paul, as he challenged Jewish and Gentile people to look beyond their cultural boundaries to see where God was breaking forth a new reality and a new people as the New Creation that lived into God's Reign. Our theology has its roots in the ministry of Saint Francis of Assisi, who embraced the poor as beloved in Christ, and called all believers to embrace simplicity, poverty, and peace as central values in Christian discipleship. Our theology has its roots in John Wesley, who challenged the Anglican Church of his day to be in ministry with the poor, to create a connectional system of ministry so to bring resources to bear to alleviate the suffering of the poor, and spread Scriptural Holiness throughout the land for the common good of all the people in the name of Jesus. Our theology has its roots in the activism of Susan B. Anthony and Elizabeth Cady Stanton, who tirelessly worked in the 19th century for Human and Civil Rights for women and ethnic minorities in America. Our theology has its roots in the Civil Rights Movement, especially in the thought and action of Martin Luther King, Jr., Fred Shuttlesworth, Rosa Parks, and the host of saints from the African-American Church in the Birmingham area. Like Jesus and Paul and saints from throughout the history of the Christian faith, King, Shuttlesworth, and Parks called the church to a rediscovery and recommitment to the nonviolent ministry of peace of Jesus Christ against enormous violence and overwhelming odds.

Our theology of Radical Hospitality is centered on the inclusive and fully open invitation of Jesus to *all* people to enter the Reign of God. Everyone is welcome, no matter who, no matter what. Everyone, even our enemy, is seen as beloved of God. We see and experience the fullness of this invitation at the Table of Christ, where *all* people are welcome. Table fellowship was central to Jesus, and Table fellowship is central to Church of the Reconciler. Each Sunday at Church of the Reconciler, we celebrate Holy Communion, and after worship we enjoy the fellowship of a Common Meal. As in the New Testament, these two realities of Eucharist and Common Meal are not only side by side, but are often one and the same. As we explore Holy Communion and Common Meal, I think it is too narrow a focus to consider the Last Supper as the only event that impacts our understanding of the meaning of Holy Communion and Common Meal in Christian tradition. For us to understand the fullness of what Holy Communion and Common Meal are about, we must see both in light of the full ministry of Jesus, especially *all the other meals* experienced with our Lord, especially those with the outcast and marginalized. Again, it is important to consider what we have learned from John Dominic Crossan, who describes Jesus' ministry as a ministry of "open commensality" where a radical hospitality is shown by Jesus to everyone at whatever table he might share. [124] Jesus ate with everyone. He shared the table with outcast and sinner, Pharisee and Zealot, the rich and the poor. Everyone was welcome. Over and again we read stories of Jesus eating and welcoming and showing with his radical hospitality what the Reign of God can be about.

Also, we must read the many stories in the Gospels of Jesus feeding the thousands as references to Jesus' meal practice, informing us as to how we are to understand Holy Communion and Common Meal. Certainly, these are "Eucharistic" experiences. Jesus is feeding people, body and soul, the Bread of Heaven. *Everyone* who comes is fed. All are welcome. There is no entrance exam or segregation of those who are "worthy" or "unworthy." It is also noteworthy that Jesus feed the thousands on *both* sides of the Sea of Galilee, the Gentile and the Jew. No one is turned away. This concept is especially important as we consider the question of "Open Communion." If Jesus fed the Bread of Heaven to the thousands, the clean and unclean, the Jew and Gentile, those who have committed themselves to Jesus, as well as those who are just "on-lookers," then should we not do the same? All of these stories of meal and feeding in the Gospels and the Epistles point to an avalanche of evidence that Jesus' ministry was about "open commensality." This is certainly the reason behind the tradition in the New Testament of the Common

Meal as the place where thanksgiving, "Eucharist," happened. This is the theological center of Radical Hospitality at Church of the Reconciler: Holy Communion and Common Meal. What we do at the Table tells everything about Church of the Reconciler.

Our theology of Radical Hospitality is expressed equally in Word, Sacrament, and Ministry. What is said and done at the Pulpit and Table then moves to the street. What we learn, experience, and receive at the Table, we live out on the street: The Radical Hospitality at the Table gives to all the grace and peace of God in Jesus Christ, and is then lived out in a Social Gospel commitment of Prophetic Nonviolence.

Teaching Principles of Nonviolence

Just as Martin Luther King, Jr. and the other saints who led the Nonviolent Movement in the struggle for Civil Rights discovered, living a life of Prophetic Nonviolence without intense discipline, and unwavering commitment is impossible. Just as the leaders who sought to integrate the lunch counters, restrooms, and schools in Birmingham in the 1960's had to be well trained in the principles of nonviolence, the church that seeks to work with the poor and the outcast in our culture of violence must be well trained in living out Gospel nonviolence. Every day at Church of the Reconciler, we discover again and again that nonviolence is the only path for our ministry. Each day hundreds of desperate, angry, hungry, abused people walk through our doors. The violence of our culture has been dumped upon them and by them in loads far beyond ordinary understanding, loads too heavy to bear. Vengeance, retribution, and/or self-hatred are lying just below the surface. Thus, violence can explode upon anyone who triggers an outburst. The only way we can be in ministry at Church of the Reconciler is to practice disciplined, intentional nonviolence. For our staff, any flash of anger, any authoritarian demand, any judgmental response could trigger anger and violence that could be lethal for ourselves or others in the building. We simply do not know what burdens the homeless bear. Unless we have walked in their shoes, we cannot understand or predict what their pain will push them to do. Every person who walks through our doors has endured great loss, great sorrow, great betrayal, and almost certainly great violence.

At Church of the Reconciler, we have made a commitment to teaching principles of nonviolence in every area of our ministry. A great blessing for our congregation has been the assistance of well trained, gifted leaders in nonviolence: Dr. Sis Levin and her husband Jerry Levin are active participants in our congregation, teaching principles of nonviolence. Sis and Jerry have devoted their lives to teaching nonviolence, and have done so around the world. Sis Levin is an educator, teaching others how to teach nonviolence; and Jerry Levin was a journalist, the CNN Middle East Bureau Chief for several years. Jerry was taken hostage by religious extremists while working in the Middle East; and Sis worked behind the scenes to affect his release. Later, Sis and Jerry were missionaries, supported by Cathedral Church of the Advent in Birmingham (Episcopal), teaching nonviolence in Bethlehem in Palestine. In the course of their life experiences, Sis and Jerry have produced a curriculum and process of teaching nonviolence in schools and churches. We teach these principles of nonviolence to our children, youth, and adults. We preach these principles of nonviolence from the pulpit, and express the fullness of them at the Communion Table. These principles embody a spiritual life-commitment to nonviolence. They are action-oriented responses that help focus our thought processes toward nonviolent relationships and resolutions.

Principles of Nonviolence

1. Eliminate All Disrespect

2. Recognize and Congratulate Others

3. Choose and Consult Wise People

4. Acknowledge Hurts

5. Heal Wounds

Although intentionally designed to be used in a multi-faith environment, each one of these principles is directly related to the teachings of Jesus. In every Bible Study, in every Sunday School lesson taught, in every story told to illustrate the truth of the faith at Church of the Reconciler, we encourage a reflection upon how these principles of nonviolence are employed. These principles provide an interpretive lens through which we can see more clearly and saturate more deeply the nonviolent way of Jesus and respond in a more Christ-like way in the midst of the injustice, pain, and crisis we encounter. The more we hear and remember these principles of nonviolence, the more *resilient* we will be in the face of violence to respond in a Christ-like, nonviolent way that builds understanding, reconciliation, and peace.

Radical Hospitality For Gay and Lesbian People

It is in this same context, with this same theology, that we embrace the gay and lesbian people of downtown Birmingham. Lesbian and gay people come to Church of the Reconciler. This fact, in and of itself, is remarkable. Even after centuries of being shunned and mistreated as "incompatible" with the community that is the church, gay and lesbian people still come. Why? Perhaps it is because in the midst of growing up in a church that rejects who they are, they heard the message and read the stories of liberation, forgiveness, reconciliation, redemption, and salvation that have power and meaning beyond the pain of how they have been treated. Perhaps they encountered the living Christ and God's grace in the midst of the broken, fragile, and incomplete community that is the church. For whatever reason, gay and lesbian people come.

Some lesbian and gay people come to Church of the Reconciler because they have heard about our ministry in downtown Birmingham. They might have experienced the Radical Hospitality of our ministry through volunteering to work beside the homeless with another group or church; they might have experienced our ministry through the Birmingham Peace Project, or some other ecumenical or multi-faith gathering that took place here. Through a number of avenues, the gay community interacts with our congregation, and because of the hospitality experienced here, lesbian and gay people come back.

The diversity of the homosexual population is as equally diverse as the heterosexual majority. We greet at Church of the Reconciler lesbian and gay people from every social strata of our society. Middle class people from the gay community, both "closeted" and "out" individuals, participate fully in our congregation. Their full welcome, our shared Radical Hospitality, and their inclusion as open and full participants and leaders in our church are a blessing for our congregation.

We also greet and welcome many homeless gay and lesbian people. For many of these individuals, their sexuality is a central contributing factor in their homelessness. Many young adult homosexuals, 21 to 35 years of age, whom we meet are homeless because of the rejection and expulsion they experienced from their family. [125] Although HIV/AIDS is now an issue as equally predominant among poor African-Americans as it is among the gay community, the effect of HIV/AIDS has specific consequences for gay men. Many gay men are homeless because of medical issues related to HIV/AIDS. Without significant financial and emotional support from family, if a person is gay and sick with HIV/AIDS, and has no medical insurance, the financial, emotional, and spiritual burden quickly leads to poverty and homelessness. All of these issues of oppression and rejection, including the spiritual violence of the church, devastates the lives of gay and lesbian people and often leads to homelessness. [126] These are the people we often welcome into Church of the Reconciler. Their participation and servant leadership in our church, especially considering the context of their suffering, is a blessing and witness for our congregation of the depth of their faith.

How do we welcome homosexual people? We enthusiastically embrace them with the Radical Hospitality of Jesus, and we live out our Christ-centered Principles of Nonviolence:

Principle I: Eliminate All Disrespect

The first encounter we typically have with a visitor is through either our Sunday Worship or our daily Common Meal. At both of these events, we as a staff and as a church are very intentional in expressing this basic value of Jesus' Radical Hospitality in all that we say and do: Everyone is given full respect as a beautiful creation of God, created in the image of God. In our music, in our welcome, in our "passing of the peace," in our preaching, in our "open table" at Holy Communion, and our invitation to membership, we are "over the top" in emphasizing the complete welcome and complete respect for all people at Church of the Reconciler: "No matter who, no matter what," everyone born of a woman is fully loved by God, and is invited to full membership and participation in this church: Black, White, Brown, Rich, Poor, Gay, Straight... everyone is welcomed by Jesus, who is our host. For many lesbian and gay people, they have heard the slogan that "everyone is welcome" many times; however, there is always an undercurrent "exception" in most churches they have attended: "Everyone is welcome *except* homosexual people." In our congregation, we fully respect homosexual people and all their relationships. Our hospitality is enthusiastically, vocally announced. At Church of the Reconciler, homosexual people are welcome to come with their partner and openly be a part of our church family with their *whole* family.

This Radical Hospitality must be intentionally, willfully expressed. We as a church and staff cannot assume that "everybody gets it." For all people, but especially those people on the margins of our society, unless the enthusiastic expression of Radical Hospitality and its inherent *full respect* of all people is made abundantly, vocally clear, many people on the margins will assume they are not *fully* welcome because of their experiences of the past.

Principle II: Recognize and Congratulate Others

We recognize lesbian and gay people as being fully human, with full integrity. We accept them as whole persons as they are. We recognize and congratulate the spiritual journey of gay and lesbian people: They are spiritual champions who have endured the suffering they have experienced and continue to be people full of faith and hope.

Our staff, both lay and clergy, and our membership have a clear understanding that the center of all that we do is the Lord's Table. The Lord's Table is both the Communion Table and the Common Meal Table. For us, these are intimately connected. Both are sacramental. At both, Jesus is present. We, with Christ, welcome people, feed people, and dine with people. It is in the breaking of the bread, the nourishment of body, mind, and spirit, and the sharing of our common journey where we are truly vulnerable and open to one another. This is the Emmaus story, happening again and again: At the breaking of the bread we see Christ in the midst of the stranger. At the table, we listen to each other. We see in each other's eyes the pain and joy. At Church of the Reconciler, at every meal, the staff join in table fellowship with all who enter the church. We recognize, listen, and congratulate *everyone*. It is in the listening, recognizing, and congratulating one another where gay and lesbian people know that they are in a safe place where they are taken seriously as people of God. This is the place where the first steps toward mutual healing with our homosexual brothers and sisters can take place. This is the place where honesty, reconciliation, and peace can begin.

Principle III: Choose and Consult Wise People

At Church of the Reconciler, we are very straightforward and direct in our advice: Do not continue destructive relationships. If a person has a destructive relationship with drugs or alcohol, we intervene as directly as possible to encourage a change towards recovery. We host recovery meetings with Alcoholics Anonymous in our facility, and we regularly connect principles of recovery with principles of Christian discipleship in our Bible Study and topical Study Meetings. We introduce and connect people to wise, experienced people who understand what recovery is about. If a person is engaging in destructive sexual practices, we intervene as directly as possible, strongly encouraging the person to stop, change, and live a life of nonviolence toward self and others. Likewise, if a person is in a relationship that is destructive either emotionally or spiritually, we are very direct in our recommendation: First, disassociate yourself from all communities of spiritual and emotional violence so that healing can begin. Many gay and lesbian people come out of families and communities of intense spiritual violence toward homosexual people. Many people have been "discipled" by spiritual leaders who proclaim an authoritarian shame-filled theology that is toxic to lesbian and gay people. Homosexual people from across the social spectrum, middle-class and homeless, come through the doors of Church of the Reconciler deeply burdened and wounded by shame-based theologies from churches who treat homosexuals as "incompatible," sick, or even "condemned to hell" simply because they are gay. Many lesbian and gay individuals have physically left these environments, but have not emotionally and spiritually left the theologies that feed these environments. Our goal is to introduce these gay and lesbian people to theological points of view that express the larger diversity found in the Christian faith, especially ones from the "underside" of history, written from the margins and by minorities, like those found in this book. Church of the Reconciler continues to sponsor workshops and Study Series which open new possibilities for many in their understanding of sexuality, nonviolence, and a fearless Social Gospel interpretation of our world. Our goal at Church of the Reconciler is to introduce shame-based homosexual people to other people who have already made the journey out of shame-based spirituality. Our goal is to offer another vision of who we can be as Christians by building a community of Radical Hospitality and Christ-like nonviolence where all who enter can find a spiritual home. Our goal is to introduce and connect people to wise, spiritually mature people who welcome the homosexual person as fully Christian.

However, this Nonviolence Principle of "Choose and Consult Wise People" has much more to say to the wider church than to anyone else. It is the church, for its own sake, and for the sake of God's Reign, that needs to choose and consult wise people who are gay and lesbian. The church has failed to choose homosexual people as leaders and clergy. This violence done to ourselves has deeply wounded the witness of the Gospel. Consider for a moment the many, many people full of deep wisdom, gifts of creativity and leadership in every area of need who have been pushed out and rejected simply because they are gay. In my own life I have personally known dozens of individuals with gifts and graces for ministry who have been forced out of church leadership for *no reason except for their sexuality.* How many do you know? How many has the church thrown out? We cannot count the number. We have failed to choose and consult these wise people. It is our loss that is the greatest.

Principle IV: Acknowledge Hurts

Many, many people who walk through the doors at Church of the Reconciler have endured great loss, great sorrow, great betrayal, and almost certainly great violence. Many walk in like zombies, drained of all emotion and sensitivity. Many have been beaten down physically, emotionally, and spiritually to the point that they have lost the will to reflect upon anything other than their immediate survival. Some of these people are homeless; some are middle-class. Some are suffering from addiction; some are suffering from circumstances beyond their control. Most of these individuals are heterosexual; some of these individuals are homosexual. For all of these individuals, it takes time and a "safe" relationship before a level of trust can be built where a person can open up about their journey and its pain. For lesbian and gay people, there is the additional uncertainty: How will they be judged by myself or other clergy if they reveal that they are homosexual? Because of rejection felt from churches and religious leaders in the past, this question is always present for homosexual people. There are many barriers for gay and lesbian people to overcome before they can open up and discuss honestly the hurt and pain they have endured, especially with "mainline" clergy who represent religious institutions that reject homosexual people. And so, we in the church must model this behavior of confession if we expect to see and hear it from the wounded who walk through our doors. We must confess our wounds, both those we have inflicted, and those under which we continue to suffer. We must weep, confess, and repent, not only for our own souls, but also to show others the path toward hope and wholeness. Until we are rigorously honest about the hurts and harm we experience and participate in, we will never move through them together toward healing.

The hurts we must acknowledge about the church and its relationship with homosexual people must be holistic, addressing every concentric circle of our life: 1) Our relationship with God, and our understanding of God's atonement, redemption and salvation. 2) The intimate and personal, which includes how the church has punished homosexual people by refusing to honor and bless the relationships of lesbian and gay people. 3) The social relationships in communities of faith and in networks of employment, including the violence done to homosexual people in discrimination and bigotry by institutions of society. 4) The political and global: The violence and oppression of homosexual people by governments around the world, where the church is complicit through its policies of dehumanizing rejection. We must be rigorously honest about what has been done. By God's grace, the truth about ourselves will begin the movement of the Holy Spirit that will set all of us free.

Principle V: Heal Wounds

Healing is our goal at Church of the Reconciler. We are rigorously honest about what we see and hear. We practice Radical Hospitality and Prophetic Nonviolence. These are our only roads to healing. Healing is a process; it is a journey as much as it is a destination. This process of being restored to bodily wholeness, emotional well-being, mental functioning, spiritual aliveness, and social holiness is central to our understanding of redemption and salvation. Our understanding of healing is a "this world" redemption and salvation in Jesus Christ. This holiness that we speak of refers to a sense of personal unity and integration of one's self in a life-giving dynamic relationship to God, world, and community. Thus, healing and salvation are linked in that they both involve restoration to dynamic wholeness in body, mind, spirit, society and the world in proper relation to God. [127]

Our understanding of healing is intimately related to atonement with God. Throughout this book I have focused on the importance of our Christian understanding of atonement and its impact on self, church, community, society. Atonement is literally being "At One" with God, neighbor, and self. Atonement is living in a life-giving, dynamic relationship where body, mind, spirit, society, and the world are understood and lived out in the proper relationship of God's grace. This being "At One" is centered on the work of God in Jesus Christ, who in grace welcomes us in Radical Hospitality and teaches us the Prophetic Nonviolent Gospel, and calls us into the Reign of God, on earth as it is in heaven. Our understanding of atonement is fully in sync with the Wesleyan Tradition. This atonement is understood, accepted, lived-out in a life of Sanctification where we are "going on to perfection" in God's grace in Jesus Christ. This process of Sanctification is living a life in the atoning grace of

God, being restored to bodily wholeness, emotional well-being, mental functioning, spiritual aliveness, and social holiness in the community of faith following Jesus Christ.

It is our assertion, based upon our understanding of Scripture, Tradition, Reason, and Experience, that lesbian and gay people are whole people, created in the image of God, and can fully participate in the sanctified life as disciples of Jesus Christ *as* homosexual people. Gay and lesbian people do not need to "healed" of their homosexuality; even the suggestion of this is absurd. Gay and lesbian people need to be healed from the wounds and sin they carry from their struggle with the sin and violence of this world in the same way that heterosexual people need to be healed.

At Church of the Reconciler we are passionately devoted to welcoming, proclaiming, facilitating, and celebrating a healing process of redemption, salvation, and sanctification in a Social Gospel ministry for *all* people. Each day we welcome stranger and friend, and offer ourselves in servant ministry, providing multiple avenues of social/spiritual ministry.

Many of the ways, large and small, that we practice Radical Hospitality and Prophetic Nonviolence for homosexual people which lead to healing have been documented here. For me, however, the most important, the most holistic healing action at Church of the Reconciler is the healing that takes place for gay and lesbian people in the sacramental life of the congregation. It is through the sacraments of the church, and the sacramental life of the congregation, that people, at the depth of their being, understand grace, embrace grace, are embraced by the community of grace, and choose to live a life of grace following Jesus Christ. In our life as Christians, healing and the sacramental life cannot be separated.

Sacramental Hospitality

We are a church. We are not a "social service agency," where individuals come as consumers to get what they want/need. We are not part of a government bureaucracy, where people are entitled to goods and services paid for through taxation. We are not a "social club," where individuals are welcomed based upon class, wealth, or privilege. We are the church. We are the Body of Christ, with many members, many gifts, all being healed by the same Spirit. We are a church, sharing the sacramental life, seeking the Reign of God. It is the sacraments, celebrated in the life of the church, which define who we are and whose we are. The sacraments of Holy Communion and Baptism are signs of God's grace, celebrated by the community of faith, as praise and remembrance of what God has done for us, as the joy of the presence of God in our lives today, and as hope in the future, which God holds for us. This living memory, this joy of our identity, this hope in God's future is grounded in our experience of God's grace as it was and is shared in the life and teachings, the death and resurrection of Jesus Christ. By participating in the sacramental life of the church, we are *all* named, claimed, taught, fed, healed, serve, married, buried, and ushered into life eternal, all by the power of the Spirit. The sacraments serve to identify Christ's meaning for these human realities, and to invite people to choose that meaning over other, less creative, healing, and nourishing meanings that are possible. [128] The sacraments do not take place in isolation from life as a dead ritual. It is through participation in the ritual and embracing its meaning over and again that cognitively and viscerally brings people into the experience of the saving action of Jesus Christ: We hear, touch, taste, and feel Jesus at work in the church. At the heart of the sacramental life is our connection, our "communion" with the divine reality of the Reign of God, on earth as it is in heaven, as we celebrate these sacraments. One traditional phrase defining the sacraments has been "means of grace." John Wesley called them "outward signs, words, or actions ordained by God to be the ordinary channels through which prevenient, justifying, and sanctifying grace are conveyed to us." [129] In the believers' participation in the sacramental life is sanctification: The growing into this new meaning, purpose, and vocation defines our life. The meaning of the sacraments in the life of the believer build power, confidence, and boldness in the community of faith to live out the love and service proclaimed in the Gospel. To embrace the identity and meaning of the sacraments through regular worship and participation allows believers to "put on" the way of Jesus over and again with a commitment to Radical Hospitality and Prophetic Nonviolence in the life of the church's ministry. The sacramental life is about hospitality and peace: It is an invitation to live in faith, hope, and love with brothers and sisters in Christ. The sacramental life, lived out in the ritual and ministry of the church, allows people the freedom to meet their God and be drawn where God wills to lead them. The sacramental ministry of the church is a healing ministry: It is a poetic ministry, inviting, not imposing. We are healed in this communion with grace. [130]

My experience has shown me that the celebration of the sacraments and their emphasis in the life of the church has been especially important in the spiritual life of gay and lesbian people. Could this be because of their life in isolation as outcasts? Because the sacraments are so much about invitation, hospitality, communion, and healing, these experiences and affirmations in the life of the church are especially precious to people who have been cast aside. The sacraments are about being included.

The sacramental life is so profound for the life of the church because the sacraments have a great depth of meaning on many different levels of our experience. They are each a multi-faceted expression of how God's healing grace is present in our lives. Throughout this book I have emphasized the importance of Radical Hospitality as an essential value and blessing in the sacramental life. However, there is much more: As memory, as identity, as offering, as an act that unifies us, as the call for liberation and social justice, and as the promise of God's future, the sacraments define who we are as followers of Jesus Christ. [131] For lesbian and gay people, this multi-faceted experience of God's grace heals in ways specific to their situation. In the following discussion, I will explore different aspects of how I have experienced the sacramental life as a healing presence in the life of homosexual people, using the categories of understanding the

sacramental life found in Horton Davies book,
"Bread of Life and Cup of Joy."

Memory

Baptism is an act of worship which reminds us that God loved us before we were even aware. Before we can make a choice, before we can even reject it, God's ever-present grace has chosen us and is always for us. In the Anglican Tradition in the United Methodist Church, we baptize infants. In the language of John Wesley, we do so because of God's "Prevenient grace." God does not wait for us to respond before beginning to work within us. Without this emphasis on grace, the memory of Baptism becomes more centered on what we do, rather than a memory of gratitude for what God has done for us.

In the Eucharist, we literally "Do this in remembrance of me": In remembrance of God's self-giving love in the life, death, and resurrection of Jesus Christ. It is a powerful memory of the center point of history when God's Word was made flesh in the life of Jesus Christ. It is a memory of the new covenant, the new relationship of God and humanity grounded in the grace of Jesus Christ.

For gay and lesbian people, the power of Jesus' Radical Hospitality and prophetic ministry to the shunned and outcast is remembered over and again in each celebration of Baptism and Holy Communion. Remembering is the human center of the sacramental life, where we remember being included in the household of faith and are part of the family of God. The very heart of the liturgy is *anamnesis*, a term derived from 1 Corinthians 11:24, where we commemorate or recall past events so that they are made present through their effects. This remembering, this memory of being welcomed by Jesus, is precious to those who have been abandoned and abused.

Identity

In Baptism is proclaimed the Christian identity: A child of God. God has loved us and has chosen us. We are God's own. As baptized people of God we profess that it is God who has saved us and not we ourselves. We profess that we are broken and sinful people who have been redeemed by God's grace in Jesus Christ. We are part of the Body of Christ, an ever present witness to the grace of God in the world.

In the Eucharist, we celebrate this identity and are nourished in our faith as we remind one another of who we are as the Body of Christ. As the disciples reflected upon their own experience of their last supper with Jesus, his death and resurrection, there was birthed within them a new identity of who they were and whom God called them to be. As the early church shared its common meal and supported one another in loving fellowship, they affirmed one another as a community of equals who were loved and valued by God and empowered by the Holy Spirit. As we experience the service of Holy Communion in worship, we clarify and affirm within our own journey that we are a part of the Body of Christ. We renew our understanding of whom the grace of God calls us to be, as individuals, as a congregation, and as the church universal.

Identity is about a person and a culture's self understanding at the very depth of their being. For homosexual people, being grounded and rooted in the sacramental life means being reminded over and again through acts of worship that their identity is not "incompatible" with Christian teaching. Their identity is not "sick" or inherently "sinful." They are whole persons, loved fully by God and welcomed fully in the life of the church. Their identity is firmly rooted in the Christian life in their redemption, salvation, and sanctification as disciples of Jesus Christ. In the words of St. Paul: "If God is for us, who can be against us?" (Romans 8:31)

Offering

In the act of baptism, the church offers an outward sign of the unmerited, undeserved grace of God. It is an offering of the hope of salvation to humanity. This offering, grounded in God's grace is also from the congregation. The congregation offers itself to the one baptized, that it will be there for them as a nurturing community of faith that will support and cherish the one presented. The person baptized makes an offering, either for themselves or for the child being brought forth, that they will offer themselves as a living witness to what God has done in their life, through their participation in the life of the church. Baptism is not an individual act. It is an offering of God within a community of faith that is symbolic of what God has offered for all humanity-- grace.

The Eucharist is the self-giving offering of God through the person of Jesus Christ. Jesus lived, taught, died, and was raised to new life as an offering unto us, so that we could know God. The Eucharist is a celebration of the passion God has for us, to give us this gift of grace, the embodiment of The Word. And as God has offered God-self to us, we are called in the eating of the bread and drinking of the wine, to offer ourselves for others as a living sacrifice to a holy life.

As God has offered grace upon grace as gift and offering to us through the experience of the sacraments, homosexual people are affirmed that this gift of grace has been given to them in full portion along with everyone else. Further, gay and lesbian people are affirmed that just as they have received, so they can and will give. In my own ministry I have been blessed over and again by the servant ministry of homosexual people in the life of the church. Lesbian and gay people have poured out offerings and gifts, many times in the midst of silent suffering as they have been pushed into silent service because of the homophobia of the church. In the sacramental life, homosexual people are affirmed that they have many gifts, and these gifts they have offered with great courage in the most difficult of circumstances by the power of the Spirit.

Liberation and Social Justice

The grace of God given to us is our forgiveness of sin and empowerment by the Spirit to seek the Reign of God. The forgiveness of sin liberates us from the bondage of the powers of this world and calls us to new relationship of justice, peace, and love within the Reign of God. The act of baptism is the celebration within the community of faith of the forgiveness of our sin and the new relationship we have with God and with others. We are called as God's people to be a new creation, and bring into this world the Reign of God. Every time the ritual of Baptism is celebrated, it is a call for the whole church to include all people in its ministry, seeking justice and nonviolent peace for all people. Baptism is a commission for the believer to go into the world for Christ seeking the Reign of God.

The Eucharist is a feast of joy that the church shares and wishes others to share, that celebrates the brotherhood and sisterhood of all humanity in Christ. It is a celebration of the earthly banquet, remembering the Passover liberation meal, and the Lord's Supper, but also the heavenly banquet prepared for all, which offers us a vision of all of God's people surrounding the heavenly table of Jesus Christ. The very foundation of liberation and social justice is the forgiveness of sin and the empowerment for new life found in the self-giving love of God expressed in the communion meal. True communion with God and with others presupposes the abolition of all injustice and exploitation. The communion meal is the invitation and celebration of the church of the will of God for justice, peace, and fellowship of all humanity.

For gay and lesbian people, the celebration of the sacraments is a call and reminder for the church to be about the liberation of all people, and especially for homosexual people. This liberation and the spiritual revolution that brings it forth is a nonviolent revolution of God's grace. What will bring about the liberation of lesbian and gay people in the church and society is not an attack on the church, but a conversion of the church, within the church, by the power of the Holy Spirit. It is through the grace-filled suffering of nonviolent service that the hearts of believers will be changed. By faithfully living the sacramental life, homosexual people, and their friends and allies, will not be motivated by hate, or revenge, or retribution. It is in worship that our hearts are continually transformed. Through the sacramental life, following the nonviolent Christ, we will love our enemy and prayerfully work in the power of the Holy Spirit for repentance, rebirth, and reconciliation.

Promise of God's Future

The sacrament of baptism is the celebration of the new heaven and new earth, the Reign of God in our midst. It is an eschatological event. It is the celebration of the bringing forth of a new reality in the life of the person presented, and for the congregation. As people of faith, we boldly claim that the future is God's, and that the fulfillment experienced in the grace of Jesus Christ is "first fruits" of this new reality, celebrated in Baptism now, that all creation yearns to share.

In the Eucharist, the Last Supper begins with echoes of the Passover experience, but moves beyond it. As the Passover was the dark night before the liberation from Egypt, the Last Supper is a moment of self-giving grace from God that heralds the New Heaven and New Earth, even in the midst of oppression. It opens up a vision of how God will bring forth completion and redemption of all creation, in God's own time. It is the eschatological celebration of God, bringing forth a new reality, the Reign of God, on earth as it is in heaven. The celebration of the Eucharist points beyond itself to a new realm, which we share in now, but will be fulfilled in God's future.

For homosexual people, in the celebration of the sacraments, there is experienced for a moment the church as it should be, where everyone in the presence of God is understood as beloved. In the sacramental moment is celebrated the vision of the completion of creation, which God has revealed in the Risen Christ. All Christians know that we are mortal creatures who will pass through this veil of tears into the fullness of God's eternal light. In this faith is the confidence that God is with us; that nothing can separate us from the love of God. In this faith, gay and lesbian people are strengthened to live as beloved in God in a church culture that can be very oppressive. In doing this, we live out the Beatitudes together:

[3] *"Blessed are the poor in spirit, for theirs is the kingdom of heaven.*
[4] *"Blessed are those who mourn, for they will be comforted.*
[5] *"Blessed are the meek, for they will inherit the earth.*
[6] *"Blessed are those who hunger and thirst for righteousness, for they will be filled.*

[7] "Blessed are the merciful, for they will receive mercy.

[8] "Blessed are the pure in heart, for they will see God.

[9] "Blessed are the peacemakers, for they will be called children of God.

[10] "Blessed are those who are persecuted for righteousness" sake, for theirs is the
          kingdom of heaven.

[11] "Blessed are you when people revile you and persecute you and utter all kinds of
          evil against you falsely on my account. [12] Rejoice and be glad, for your reward is
          great in heaven, for in the same way they persecuted the prophets who were
          before you.

Matthew 5:3-11

CONCLUSION

What a remarkable and fruitful blessing it has been for me to be in ministry throughout my career with lesbian and gay people. Many times the Holy Spirit has been a work, leading me to new and deeper relationships with homosexual people and their friends and allies. While in college and seminary, deep friendships were made with lesbian and gay people who opened my eyes to a community hidden by our culture. Pivotal in my own spiritual development was my participation in the Committee to Study Homosexuality within the United Methodist Church. For four years I had the opportunity to experience and relate with homosexual persons from a variety of cultures and settings, not only in this country, but around the world. I was able to meet many people, with many points of view, on their own terms, not on the terms dictated by the suspicion of our mainstream "churched" culture. I was able to become close friends with gay, lesbian, liberal, conservative Christians, and was profoundly blessed by their spirituality, their warmth and compassion, their wisdom and pain. Seeing all of these people as they are, I was able to understand the unity we have in Jesus Christ.

Ever since this time with the Study Committee, I have increased my participation in communities of support for and with homosexual persons. I have learned much from gay and lesbian persons as they struggle in a religious culture that is truly oppressive and resistant to their presence. Perhaps the most amazing, most shocking reality is that many of these gay and lesbian Christians have refused to be driven away or minimized in the life of the church. Their faith, witness, and testimony in the midst of the spiritual, emotional, and physical violence that has been let loose upon them by the institution of the church is remarkable. It has been a particular blessing to participate in Affirmation, the first group in the United Methodist Church to organize nationally for the liberation of lesbian and gay people; the Reconciling Congregation Movement in the United Methodist Church; and to have active participation in Integrity, the Episcopal fellowship of gay and lesbian persons.

Through my experience, led by the Holy Spirit in the life of the church, here is what I have come to believe: In the church, if we are faithful to the ministry of Jesus, the witness of all the evidence before us, and the guidance of the Holy Spirit, then we will welcome gay and lesbian people as whole persons. For all of us today, this is a justice issue. The Gospel of Jesus Christ is that all people should be treated and honored as God's beloved, without distinction, with justice, mercy, and grace, and welcomed into the life of the church.

I have witnessed so much pain in the lives of gay and lesbian persons. My great concern is for the many people who are hurting. There are faithful, gifted gay and lesbian Christians in every church I have worked in or served as pastor. Some are in the open, others still in the "closet." All of them that I know are people with gifts of the Spirit, living lives of integrity as disciples of Jesus. All of them have been wounded, broken by the rejection they experience from the church. Gay and lesbian people become imprisoned by fear, beaten down into hiding from friends and family and church members, who have been taught by the church to judge them. Many persons, injured and broken, have left the church because of this pain. We have lost so much as persons with gifts and graces for ministry, lay and clergy, have been forced out of the church.

There are parents of gay and lesbian people in every congregation I have served, from the multi-thousand member mega-church to the small congregation of a few hundred people. Many of these parents shame themselves because they have been shamed by their church, being made to think they raised their children wrong. There are parents of gay and lesbian people who reject and condemn their own children because of the teaching of our church. This is tragic, and the church bears fault in their painful sorrow. This shame-based teaching by the church is nothing less than spiritual violence: It must stop.

We, as a church, are wrong in how we treat gay and lesbian people, their friends and allies. We should not call sinful and reject those faithful

Christians who are living in faithful relationships with integrity, with the gifts of the Spirit, living the life they were created to live. We should affirm their relationships. We should bless their covenants of life-long faithfulness and give them loving support.

In every society that has been openly studied, homosexual persons are present. They are here today...they have always been here...they always will be here. They are part of the great diversity of creation, only a misunderstood and mistreated minority. We justify our ignorance and fear of them by misusing our religious faith, and using religion as a weapon to silence and marginalize people we do not understand.

I believe one issue that motivates our church's rejection of gay and lesbian people is the fear by church leadership that the church will lose members and money if we were to be public in confronting the long-standing bias and prejudice against homosexual people that exists in our culture and in the church at large. Instead of standing with those motivated by fear, I believe the church should stand with Jesus, who stood with the marginalized, with the outcast, with the abused. Gay and lesbian people are children of God, loved by God.

By God's grace, this is where I stand; and I know I do not stand alone. There are many lay and clergy in all parts of the church who agree with me. This is not just a "regional" or "urban" issue; gay and lesbian people are in our church everywhere, forced to be "strangers" among us.

I know there are many clergy in our churches who would stand with me but for fear for their career. I pray that their fear and silence will end. I also hope that those who disagree with me on this issue will acknowledge that the position I hold is one of prayerful integrity, and is consistent with the Wesleyan theology taught in the Anglican tradition.

There is so much pain in our church over this conflict. I pray that our churches do not split over this issue; I believe the unity of the church is something that, by God's grace, can be held together in spite of significant differences. It is my commitment to speak the truth as I know it, live in peace and be a minister of the peace of Christ. I will not attack any person; and it is my hope that no one will attack me. Yet, I must do everything in my power to change the understanding of the church about homosexuality, so that what is right and true and just will be made real for gay and lesbian people. May God's grace help us all.

One in Christ

[11] So then, remember that at one time you Gentiles by birth, called "the uncircumcision" by those who are called "the circumcision"—a physical circumcision made in the flesh by human hands— [12] remember that you were at that time without Christ, being aliens from the commonwealth of Israel, and strangers to the covenants of promise, having no hope and without God in the world. [13] But now in Christ Jesus you who once were far off have been brought near by the blood of Christ. [14] For he is our peace; in his flesh he has made both groups into one and has broken down the dividing wall, that is, the hostility between us. [15] He has abolished the law with its commandments and ordinances, that he might create in himself one new humanity in place of the two, thus making peace, [16] and might reconcile both groups to God in one body through the cross, thus putting to death that hostility through it. [17] So he came and proclaimed peace to you who were far off and peace to those who were near; [18] for through him both of us have access in one Spirit to the Father. [19] So then you are no longer strangers and aliens, but you are citizens with the saints and also members of the household of God, [20] built upon the foundation of the apostles and prophets, with Christ Jesus himself as the cornerstone.

[21] *In him the whole structure is joined together and grows into a holy temple in the Lord; [22] in whom you also are built together spiritually into a dwelling place for God.*

End Notes

[1] Gary L. Ball-Kilbourne, editor, *The Church Studies Homosexuality* (Nashville: Cokesbury, 1994).

[2] *The Book of Discipline of the United Methodist Church 2008* (Nashville, TN: The United Methodist Publishing House, 2008).

[3] Martti Nissinen, *Homoeroticism in the Biblical World* (Minneapolis: Fortress Press, 1998), 16.

[4] Gary L. Ball-Kilbourne, editor, *The Church Studies Homosexuality* (Nashville: Cokesbury, 1994), 31.

[5] Mary A. Tolbert, "The Bible and Same-Gender Marriage," presented at Wisconsin's for Marriage Equality Conference, December 4, 2004 (Berkley, California: Center for Lesbian and Gay Studies of the Pacific School of Religion, 2004) http://www.cafaithforequality.org/reflect.html (accessed March 21, 2009), 2.

[6] Mary A. Tolbert, "The Bible and Same-Gender Marriage," presented at Wisconsin's for Marriage Equality Conference, December 4, 2004 (Berkley, California: Center for Lesbian and Gay Studies of the Pacific School of Religion, 2004) http://www.cafaithforequality.org/reflect.html (accessed March 21, 2009), 2.

[7] Gary L. Ball-Kilbourne, editor, *The Church Studies Homosexuality* (Nashville: Cokesbury, 1994), 48.

[8] Daniel A. Helminiak, *What the Bible Really Says About Homosexuality* (New Mexico: Alamo Square Press, 2000), 43-50; and, Jeff Miner and John Connoley, *The Children Are Free: Reexamining the Biblical Evidence on Same-Sex Relationships* (Indianapolis, Indiana: Metropolitan Press, 2001), 2-9.

[9] Gary L. Ball-Kilbourne, editor, *The Church Studies Homosexuality* (Nashville: Cokesbury, 1994), 49.

[10] Volker Sommer and Paul L. Vasey, *Homosexual Behaviour in Animals: An Evolutionary Perspective*

(Cambridge, England: Cambridge University Press, 2006), 11.

[11] John Dominic Crossan, The Historical Jesus: The Life of a Mediterranean Jewish Peasant (New York: HarperCollins Publishers, 1991), 341-344; and, Robert Funk and the Jesus Seminar, The Acts of Jesus: The Search for the Authentic Deeds of Jesus (New York: HarperSanfrancisco, 1998), 210-211.

[12] Zwi R. J. Werblowsky, "Hospitality," *The Oxford Dictionary of the Jewish Religion*, Zwi R.J. Werblowsky and Geoffrey Wigoder, editors (Oxford/New York: The Oxford University Press, 1999), 339.

[13] Zwi R.J.Werblowsky, "Hospitality," *The Oxford Dictionary of the Jewish Religion*, Zwi R.J. Werblowsky and Geoffrey Wigoder, editors (Oxford/New York: The Oxford University Press, 1999), 339.

[14] The Shabbat is the twenty-four chapter section of the Mishnah that deals specifically with activities encouraged or prohibited on the Sabbath. See Avraham Walfish, "Shabbat," in *The Oxford Dictionary of the Jewish Religion,* Zwi R.J. Werblowsky and Geoffrey Wigoder, editors (Oxford/New York: The Oxford University Press, 1999), 624.

[15] Harold V. Bennett, "Justice," *The New Interpreters Dictionary of the Bible*, edited by Katharine Doob Sakenfeld (Nashville: Abingdon Press, 2008), 476.

[16] Harold V. Bennett, "Justice," *The New Interpreters Dictionary of the Bible*, edited by Katharine Doob Sakenfeld (Nashville: Abingdon Press, 2008), 477.

[17] Dale B. Martin, *Sex and the Single Savior: Gender and Sexuality in Biblical Interpretation* (Louisville, KY: Westminster John Knox Press, 2006), 37.

[18] Dale B. Martin, *Sex and the Single Savior: Gender and Sexuality in Biblical Interpretation* (Louisville, KY: Westminster John Knox Press, 2006), 38.

[19] Martin, 38.

[20] Dale B. Martin, *Sex and the Single Savior: Gender and Sexuality in Biblical Interpretation* (Louisville, KY: Westminster John Knox Press, 2006), 39.

[21] Martin, 40.

[22] Robin Scroggs, *The New Testament and Homosexuality* (Minneapolis: Augsburg Fortress Press, 1984), 118.

[23] Robin Scroggs, *The New Testament and Homosexuality* (Minneapolis: Augsburg Fortress Press, 1984), 116-117.

[24] Dale B. Martin, *Sex and the Single Savior: Gender and Sexuality in Biblical Interpretation* (Louisville, KY: Westminster John Knox Press, 2006), 57.

[25] Victor Paul Furnish, "The Bible and Homosexuality: Reading the Texts in Context," in *Homosexuality in The Church*, edited by Jeffrey S. Siker (Louisville, KY: Westminster John Knox, 1994), 18-35.

[26] Dale B. Martin, *Sex and the Single Savior: Gender and Sexuality in Biblical Interpretation* (Louisville, KY: Westminster John Knox Press, 2006), 58; and John Dominic Crossan and Jonathan L. Reed, *In Search of Paul: How Jesus' Apostle Opposed Rome's Empire with God's Kingdom* (New York: HarperSanFranciso, 2004), 257-269.

[27] Mary A. Tolbert, "Statement for Committee on Investigation" (paper presented at a hearing held by The United Methodist Church Northern California-Nevada Annual Conference Committee on Investigation for Clergy Members, Sacramento, California, February, 2000), 2.

[28] Mary A. Tolbert, "Statement for Committee on Investigation" (paper presented at a hearing held by The United Methodist Church Northern California-Nevada Annual Conference Committee on Investigation for Clergy Members, Sacramento, California, February, 2000), 4.

[29] John Dominic Crossan, *The Historical Jesus: The Life of a Mediterranean Jewish Peasant* (New York: HarperCollins Publishers, 1991), 341-344.

[30] John Dominic Crossan, *The Historical Jesus: The Life of a Mediterranean Jewish Peasant* (New York: HarperCollins Publishers, 1991), 341-344.

[31] Mary A. Tolbert, "Statement for Committee on Investigation" (paper presented at a hearing held by The United Methodist Church Northern California-Nevada Annual Conference Committee on Investigation for Clergy Members, Sacramento, California, February, 2000), 2.

[32] Mary A. Tolbert, "Statement for Committee on Investigation" (paper presented at a hearing held by The United Methodist Church Northern California-Nevada Annual Conference Committee on Investigation for Clergy Members, Sacramento, California, February, 2000), 2.

[33] My interpretation of this text is supported in the following works: Marcus J. Borg and John Dominic Crossan, *The Last Week: A Day-by-Day Account of Jesus' Final Week in Jerusalem* (New York: HarperSanFrancisco, 2006), 31-53; Bruce J. Malina and Richard R. Rohrbaugh, *Social-Science Commentary on the Synoptic Gospels* (Minneapolis: Fortress Press, 1992), 249-253; Ched Myers, *Binding The Strong Man: A Political Reading of Mark's Story of Jesus* (Maryknoll, New York: Orbis Press, 1988), 297-304.

[34] Ched Myers, *Binding The Strong Man: A Political Reading of Mark's Story of Jesus* (Maryknoll, New York: Orbis Press, 1988), 301.

[35] Ched Myers, *Binding The Strong Man: A Political Reading of Mark's Story of Jesus* (Maryknoll, New York: Orbis Press, 1988), 301.

[36] Dwight W. Vogel, "Homosexuality and the Church: Evangelical Commitment and Prophetic Responsibility," in *The Loyal Opposition: Struggling With the Church on Homosexuality,* edited by Tex Sample and Amy E. DeLong (Nashville: Abingdon Press, 2000), 61.

[37] Joeseph Monti, *Arguing About Sex: The Rhetoric of Christian Sexual Morality* (Albany, NY: State University of New York Press, 1995), 130.

[38] Frank Leslie Cross, "Atonement," *The Oxford Dictionary of The Christian Church*, edited by F. L. Cross and E. A. Livingstone (Oxford/New York: The Oxford University Press, 1997), 123.

[39] Baruch J. Schwartz, "Sacrifices," *The Oxford Dictionary of The Jewish Religion*, edited by Zwi R.J. Werblowsky and Geoffrey Wigoder (Oxford/New York: The Oxford University Press, 1999), 598.

[40] Baruch J. Schwartz, "Sacrifices," *The Oxford Dictionary of The Jewish Religion*, edited by Zwi R.J. Werblowsky and Geoffrey Wigoder (Oxford/New York: The Oxford University Press, 1999), 598.

[41] Frank Leslie Cross, "Atonement," *The Oxford Dictionary of The Christian Church*, edited by F. L. Cross and E. A. Livingstone (Oxford/New York: The Oxford University Press, 1997), 122.

[42] Frank Leslie Cross, "Atonement," *The Oxford Dictionary of The Christian Church*, edited by F. L. Cross and E. A. Livingstone (Oxford/New York: The Oxford University Press, 1997), 123.

[43] Cross, 123.

[44] Cross, 123.

[45] Gustaf Aulen, *Christus Victor* (M.A. Eugene, Oregon: Wipf and Stock Publishers, 1931), 4.

[46] Frank Leslie Cross, "Atonement," *The Oxford Dictionary of The Christian Church*, edited by F. L. Cross and E. A. Livingstone (Oxford/New York: The Oxford University Press, 1997), 123.

[47] Saint Anselm, *Cur Deus Homo* (Chicago: Open Court Publishing Company, 1903).

[48] Cross, 123.

[49] Gustaf Aulen, *Christus Victor* (M.A. Eugene, Oregon: Wipf and Stock Publishers, 1931), 96.

[50] Aulen, 96.

[51] Gustaf Aulen, *Christus Victor* (M.A. Eugene, Oregon: Wipf and Stock Publishers, 1931), 156.

[52] Gustaf Aulen, *Christus Victor* (M.A. Eugene, Oregon: Wipf and Stock Publishers, 1931).

[53] Denny J. Weaver, *The Nonviolent Atonement* (Grand Rapids, Michigan/Cambridge, U.K.: Eerdmans Publishing Company, 2001), 225.

[54] Denny J. Weaver, *The Nonviolent Atonement* (Grand Rapids, Michigan/Cambridge, U.K.: Eerdmans Publishing Company, 2001), 3.

[55] Denny J. Weaver, *The Nonviolent Atonement* (Grand Rapids, Michigan/Cambridge, U.K.: Eerdmans Publishing Company, 2001), 5.

[56] James Cone, *A Black Theology of Liberation: Twentieth Anniversary Edition* (Maryknoll, N.Y.: Orbis Books, 1990).

[57] James Cone, *God of the Oppressed* (Maryknoll, N.Y.: Orbis Books, 1997).

[58] James Cone, *God of the Oppressed* (Maryknoll, N.Y.: Orbis Books, 1997), 57.

[59] James Cone, *God of the Oppressed*, 104–105.

[60] James Cone, *God of the Oppressed* (Maryknoll, N.Y.: Orbis Books, 1997), 107.

[61] James Cone, *God of the Oppressed*, 211.

[62] James Cone, *God of the Oppressed* (Maryknoll, N.Y.: Orbis Books, 1997), 212.

[63] Denny J. Weaver, *The Nonviolent Atonement* (Grand Rapids, Michigan/Cambridge, U.K.: Eerdmans Publishing Company, 2001), 107.

[64] Rosemary Radford Ruether, *Sexism and God-Talk: Toward a Feminist Theology* (Boston: Beacon, 1983).

[65] Rosemary Radford Ruether, *Sexism and God-Talk: Toward a Feminist Theology* (Boston: Beacon, 1983), 123.

[66] Rosemary Radford Ruether, *Sexism and God-Talk: Toward a Feminist Theology* (Boston: Beacon, 1983), 135.

[67] Rosemary Radford Ruether, *Sexism and God-Talk: Toward a Feminist Theology* (Boston: Beacon, 1983), 104.

[68] Denny J. Weaver, *The Nonviolent Atonement* (Grand Rapids, Michigan/Cambridge, U.K.: Eerdmans Publishing Company, 2001), 126-145.

[69] Denny J. Weaver, *The Nonviolent Atonement* (Grand Rapids, Michigan/Cambridge, U.K.: Eerdmans Publishing Company, 2001), 128.

[70] Julie M. Hopkins, *Towards a Feminist Christology: Jesus of Nazareth, European Women, and the Christological Crisis* (Grand Rapids: Eerdmans, 1995), 50.

[71] Weaver, 163.

[72] Delores Williams, *Sisters in the Wilderness: The Challenge of Womanist God-Talk* (Maryknoll, N.Y.: Orbis Books, 1993), 161.

[73] Williams, 165.

[74] Denny J. Weaver, *The Nonviolent Atonement* (Grand Rapids, Michigan/Cambridge, U.K.: Eerdmans Publishing Company, 2001), 165.

[75] Denny J. Weaver, *The Nonviolent Atonement* (Grand Rapids, Michigan/Cambridge, U.K.: Eerdmans Publishing Company, 2001), 170.

[76] Weaver, 110.

[77] Denny J. Weaver, *The Nonviolent Atonement* (Grand Rapids, Michigan/Cambridge, U.K.: Eerdmans Publishing Company, 2001), 54.

[78] Denny J. Weaver, *The Nonviolent Atonement* (Grand Rapids, Michigan/Cambridge, U.K.: Eerdmans Publishing Company, 2001), 225.

[79] Rene Girard, *Things Hidden Since The Foundation of The World* (Stanford, California: Stanford University Press, 1987), 18.

[80] Timothy Gorringe, *God's Just Vengeance: Crime, Violence and the Rhetoric of Salvation*, Studies in Ideology and Religion, no. 9 (Cambridge, England: Cambridge University Press, 1996).

[81] Denny J. Weaver, *The Nonviolent Atonement* (Grand Rapids, Michigan/Cambridge, U.K.: Eerdmans Publishing Company, 2001), 226.

[82] Gary L. Ball-Kilbourne, editor, *The Church Studies Homosexuality* (Nashville: Cokesbury, 1994), 24.

[83] Martti Nissinen, *Homoeroticism in the Biblical World* (Minneapolis: Fortress Press, 1998), 6.

[84] Martti Nissinen, *Homoeroticism in the Biblical World* (Minneapolis: Fortress Press, 1998), 6.

[85] Nissinen, 7.

[86] Gary L. Ball-Kilbourne, editor, *The Church Studies Homosexuality* (Nashville: Cokesbury, 1994), 24.

[87] This quotation is taken from a conversation I had with Dr. Tex Sample during the deliberations of The United Methodist Committee to Study Homosexuality, November, 1990.

[88] Gary L. Ball-Kilbourne, editor, *The Church Studies Homosexuality* (Nashville: Cokesbury, 1994), 24; and, American Psychiatric Association, *Diagnostic and Statistical Manual of Mental Disorders, Fourth Edition, Text Revision* (Washington D.C.: American Psychiatric Association, 2000), 535.

[89] "American Academy of Pediatrics Policy Statement," PEDIATRICS Vol. 109, no. 2 (February 2002), 339-340.

[90] Gary L. Ball-Kilbourne, editor, *The Church Studies Homosexuality* (Nashville: Cokesbury, 1994), 28.

[91] Ball-Kilbourne, 28.

[92] Gary L. Ball-Kilbourne, editor, *The Church Studies Homosexuality* (Nashville: Cokesbury, 1994), 32.

[93] Bruce Hilton, *Can Homophobia Be Cured? Wrestling With the Questions That Challenge the Church* (Nashville: Abingdon Press, 1992), 5.

[94] Fernando F. Segovia, "Toward a Hermeneutics of Diaspora: The Hermeneutics of Otherness and Engagement," in *Reading From This Place, Volume 1, Social Location and Biblical Interpretation in the United States,* edited by Fernando F. Segovia and Mary Ann Tolbert (Minneapolis, MN: Fortress Press, 1995), 58.

[95] H. Richard Niebuhr, *The Responsible Self: An Essay in Christian Moral Philosophy* (San Francisco: Harper & Roe, Publishers, 1963), 90-107.

[96] Joeseph Monti, *Arguing About Sex: The Rhetoric of Christian Sexual Morality* (Albany, NY: State University of New York Press, 1995), 6.

[97] Edward Farley, *Deep Symbols: Their Postmodern Effacement and Reclamation* (Harrisburg, PA: Trinity Press International, 1996).

[98] Farley, 1.

[99] Edward Farley, *Deep Symbols: Their Postmodern Effacement and Reclamation* (Harrisburg, PA: Trinity Press International, 1996), 3.

[100] Peter Berger, *The Sacred Canopy: Elements of a Sociology of Religion* (New York: Anchor Books, 1990), 10.

[101] Edward Farley, *Deep Symbols: Their Postmodern Effacement and Reclamation* (Harrisburg, PA: Trinity Press International, 1996), 3.

[102] Farley, 4.

[103] Edward Farley, *Deep Symbols: Their Postmodern Effacement and Reclamation* (Harrisburg, PA: Trinity Press International, 1996), 12.

[104] Edward Farley, *Deep Symbols: Their Postmodern Effacement and Reclamation* (Harrisburg, PA: Trinity Press International, 1996), 14.

[105] Edward Farley, *Deep Symbols: Their Postmodern Effacement and Reclamation* (Harrisburg, PA: Trinity Press International, 1996), 23.

[106] Robert D. McFadden, "Gay Marriage Is Ruled Legal in Connecticut," *The New York Times*, October 11, 2008.

[107] Jesse McKinley and Kirk Johnson, "Mormons Tipped Scale in Ban on Gay Marriage," *The New York Times*, November 14, 2008.

[108] Mary A. Tolbert, "The Bible and Same-Gender Marriage," presented at Wisconsin's for Marriage Equality Conference, December 4, 2004 (Berkley, California: Center

for Lesbian and Gay Studies of the Pacific School of Religion, 2004), http://www.cafaithforequality.org/reflect.html (accessed March 21, 2009), 2.

[109] *Of Love and Justice: Toward the Civil Recognition of Same-Sex Marriage* (Toronto: The United Church of Canada, 2003).

[110] Michael Gaddis, *There Is No Crime for Those Who Have Christ: Religious Violence in the Christian Roman Empire* (Berkeley, CA: University of California Press, 2005), 68.

[111] Robert Buchanan, *Love, Honor, and Respect: How to Confront Homosexual Bias and Violence in Christian Culture* (San Jose, CA: Writers Club Press, 2000), 29.

[112] Walter Wink, *The Powers That Be: Theology for a New Millennium* (New York: Random House, 1999).

[113] Wink, *The Powers That Be: Theology for a New Millennium*, 82.

[114] John Bradshaw, *Bradshaw On: The Family* (Deerfield Beach, FL: Health Communications, Inc., 1996), 147.

[115] Bradshaw, 147.

[116] John Bradshaw, *Bradshaw On: The Family* (Deerfield Beach, FL: Health Communications, Inc., 1996), 27.

[117] Bradshaw, 2.

[118] Marilyn Bennett Alexander and James Preston, *We Were Baptized Too: Claiming God's Grace for Lesbians and Gays* (Louisville, KY: John Knox Press, 1996), 20.

[119] Robert Buchanan, *Love, Honor, and Respect: How to Confront Homosexual Bias and Violence in Christian Culture* (San Jose, CA: Writers Club Press, 2000), 2-3.

[120] The Southern Poverty Law Center was founded in 1971 as a small Civil Rights law firm. Today, SPLC is internationally known for its tolerance education programs, legal victories against white supremacists, and its tracking of hate groups. Located in Montgomery, Alabama – the birthplace of the Civil Rights Movement – the Southern Poverty Law Center was founded by Morris Dees and Joe

Levin. Its first president was Civil Rights activist Julian Bond.

[121] Walter Wink, *Jesus and Nonviolence: A Third Way* (Minneapolis: Fortress Press, 2003), 4.

[122] Martin Luther King, Jr. *A Testament of Hope: The Essential Writings and Speeches of Martin Luther King, Jr.*, edited by James M. Washington (New York: HarperCollins, 1986), 249.

[123] Glen T. Eskew, *But for Birmingham: The Local and National Movements in the Civil Rights Struggle* (Chapel Hill, NC: The University of North Carolina Press, 1997), 56.

[124] John Dominic Crossan, *The Historical Jesus: The Life of a Mediterranean Jewish Peasant* (New York: HarperCollins Publishers, 1991), 341.

[125] Amy Davidson, "Hidden Homelessness," in *Encyclopedia of Homelessness*, edited by David Levinson (Thousand Oaks, California: Sage Publications, Inc., 2004), 206.

[126] Amy Davidson, "Hidden Homelessness," in *Encyclopedia of Homelessness*, edited by David Levinson (Thousand Oaks, California: Sage Publications, Inc., 2004), 209.

[127] Larry K. Graham, "Healing," in *Dictionary of Pastoral Care and Counseling*, edited by Rodney J. Hunter (Nashville, TN: Abingdon Press, 1990), 497.

[128] Peter E. Fink, "Sacramental Theology and Pastoral Care" in *Dictionary of Pastoral Care and Counseling*, edited by Rodney J. Hunter (Nashville, TN: Abingdon Press, 1990), 1099.

[129] John Wesley, *John Wesley's Sermons: An Anthology*, edited by Albert C. Outler and Richard P. Heitzenrater (Nashville, Tennessee: Abingdon Press, 1987), 503.

[130] Peter E. Fink, "Sacramental Theology and Pastoral Care" in *Dictionary of Pastoral Care and Counseling*, edited by Rodney J. Hunter (Nashville, TN: Abingdon Press, 1990), 1099.

[131] Horton Davies, *Bread of Life and Cup of Joy* (Grand Rapids, Michigan: Eerdmans Publishing Co., 1993), 1.

BIBLIOGRAPHY

Alexander, Marilyn Bennett, and James Preston. *We Were Baptized Too: Claiming God's Grace for Lesbians and Gays*. Louisville, KY: John Knox Press, 1996.

American Psychiatric Association: *Diagnostic and Statistical Manual of Mental Disorders, Fourth Edition, Text Revision*. Washington D.C.: American Psychiatric Association, 2000.

Aulen, Gustaf. *Christus Victor*. Translated by A.G. Hebert. M.A. Eugene, Oregon: Wipf and Stock Publishers, 1931.

Ball-Kilbourne, Gary L., editor. *The Church Studies Homosexuality*. Nashville: Cokesbury, 1994.

Bawer, Bruce. *A Place At The Table, The Gay Individual in American Society*. New York: Simon and Schuster, 1993.

Bennett, Harold V. "Justice" in *The New Interpreters Dictionary of The Bible*. Edited by Katharine Doob Sakenfeld. Nashville: Abingdon Press, 2008.

Berger, Peter. *The Sacred Canopy: Elements of a Sociology of Religion*. New York: Anchor Books, 1990.

Borg, Marcus J. *Meeting Jesus Again for the First Time: The Historical Jesus and The Heart of Contemporary Faith*. New York: HarperCollins Publishers, 1994.

Borg, Marcus J., and John Dominic Crossan. *The Last Week: A Day-by-Day Account of Jesus' Final Week in Jerusalem*. New York: HarperSanFrancisco, 2006.

Boswell, John. *Christianity, Social Tolerance, and Homosexuality: Gay People in Western Europe from the Beginning of the Christian Era to the Fourteenth century.* Chicago: The University of Chicago Press, 1980.

Bradshaw, John. *Bradshaw On: The Family.* Deerfield Beach, FL: Health Communications, Inc., 1996.

Brock, Rita Nakashima. *Journeys by Heart: A Christology of Erotic Power.* New York: Crossroad, 1988.

Buchanan, Robert. *Love, Honor, and Respect: How to Confront Homosexual Bias and Violence in Christian Culture.* San Jose, CA: Writers Club Press, 2000.

Cone, James. *A Black Theology of Liberation: Twentieth Anniversary Edition.* Maryknoll, N.Y.: Orbis Books, 1990.

God of the Oppressed. Maryknoll, N.Y.: Orbis Books, 1997.

Cross, F.L., and E. A. Livingstone, editors. *The Oxford Dictionary of The Christian Church.* Oxford/New York: The Oxford University Press, 1997.

Crossan, John Dominic. *The Historical Jesus: The Life of a Mediterranean Jewish Peasant.* New York: HarperCollins Publishers, 1991.

---------*God and Empire: Jesus Against Rome Then and Now.* New York: HarperCollins Publishers, 2007.

Crossan, John Dominic, and Jonathan L. Reed. *In Search of Paul: How Jesus' Apostle Opposed Rome's Empire with God's Kingdom.* New York: HarperSanFranciso, 2004.

Davies, Horton. *Bread of Life and Cup of Joy*. Grand Rapids, Michigan: Eerdmans Publishing Co., 1993.

Davidson, Amy. "Hidden Homelessness," in *Encyclopedia of Homelessness*. Edited by Levinson, David. Thousand Oaks, California: Sage Publications, Inc., 2004.

Eskew, Glen T. *But for Birmingham: The Local and National Movements in the Civil Rights Struggle*. Chapel Hill, NC: The University of North Carolina Press, 1997.

Farley, Edward. *Deep Symbols: Their Postmodern Effacement and Reclamation*. Harrisburg, PA: Trinity Press International, 1996.

Fink, Peter E. "Sacramental Theology and Pastoral Care" in *Dictionary of Pastoral Care and Counseling*. Edited by Rodney J. Hunter. Nashville, TN: Abingdon Press, 1990.

Funk, Robert, and the Jesus Seminar. *The Acts of Jesus: The Search for the Authentic Deeds of Jesus*. New York: HarperSanfrancisco, 1998.

Furnish, Victor Paul. "The Bible and Homosexuality: Reading the Texts in Context," in *Homosexuality in The Church*. Edited by Jeffrey S. Siker. Louisville, KY: Westminster John Knox, 1994.

Gaddis, Michael. *There Is No Crime for Those Who Have Christ: Religious Violence in the Christian Roman Empire*. Berkeley, CA: University of California Press, 2005.

Geis, Sally B. and Donald E.Messer, editors. *Caught in the Crossfire*. Nashville: Abingdon Press, 1994.

Girard, Rene. *Things Hidden Since The Foundation of The World*. Translated by Steven Bann and Michael Metter. Stanford, California: Stanford University Press, 1987.

Gorringe, Timothy. *God's Just Vengeance: Crime, Violence and the Rhetoric of Salvation*, Cambridge Studies in Ideology and Religion, no. 9. Cambridge, England: Cambridge University Press, 1996.

Graham, Larry K. "Healing" in *Dictionary of Pastoral Care and Counseling*. Edited by Rodney J. Hunter. Nashville, TN: Abingdon Press, 1990.

Helminiak, Daniel A. *What the Bible Really Says About Homosexuality*. New Mexico: Alamo Square Press, 2000.

Hilton, Bruce. *Can Homophobia Be Cured? Wrestling With the Questions That Challenge the Church*. Nashville: Abingdon Press, 1992.

Hopkins, Julie M. *Towards a Feminist Christology: Jesus of Nazareth, European Women, and the Christological Crisis*. Grand Rapids: Eerdmans, 1995.

Horsley, Richard A., *Jesus and Empire: The Kingdom of God and the New World Disorder*. Minneapolis, MN: Augsburg Fortress Press, 2003.

King, Martin Luther, Jr. *A Testament of Hope: The Essential Writings and Speeches of Martin Luther King, Jr.*, Edited by James M. Washington. New York: HarperCollins, 1986.

Nissinen, Martti. *Homoeroticism in the Biblical World*. Minneapolis: Fortress Press, 1998.

Malina, Bruce J., and Richard R. Rohrbaugh. *Social-Science Commentary on the Synoptic Gospels.* Minneapolis: Fortress Press. 1992.

Martin, Dale B. *Sex and the Single Savior: Gender and Sexuality in Biblical Interpretation.* Louisville, KY: Westminster John Knox Press, 2006.

McCarthy, Emmanuel Charles. *To Teach What Jesus Taught: A Call to Fidelity.* Wilmington, DE: Center for Christian Nonviolence, 2004.

Miner, Jeff, and John Connoley. *The Children Are Free: Reexamining the Biblical Evidence on Same-Sex Relationships.* Indianapolis, Indiana: Metropolitan Press, 2001.

Monti, Joeseph. *Arguing About Sex: The Rhetoric of Christian Sexual Morality.* Albany, NY: Sate University of New York Press, 1995.

Myers, Ched. *Binding The Strong Man: A Political Reading of Mark's Story of Jesus.* Maryknoll, New York: Orbis Press, 1988.

Niebuhr, H. Richard. *The Responsible Self: An Essay in Christian Moral Philosophy.* San Francisco: Harper & Roe, Publishers, 1963.

Of Love and Justice: Toward the Civil Recognition of Same-Sex Marriage. Toronto: The United Church of Canada, 2003.

Patterson, Stephen J. *The God of Jesus: The Historical Jesus and the Search for Meaning.* Harrisburg, Pennsylvania: Trinity Press International, 1998.

Ruether, Rosemary Radford. *Sexism and God-Talk: Toward a Feminist Theology*. Boston: Beacon, 1983.

Saint Anselm. *Cur Deus Homo*. Translated by Sydney Norton Dean. Chicago: Open Court Publishing Company, 1903.

Segovia, Fernando F., "Toward a Hermeneutics of Diaspora: The Hermeneutics of Otherness and Engagement," in *Reading From This Place, Volume 1, Social Location and Biblical Interpretation in the United States*. Edited by Fernando F. Segovia and Mary Ann Tolbert. Minneapolis, MN: Fortress Press, 1995.

Scanzoni, Letha, and Virginia Ramey Mollenkott. *Is the Homosexual My Neighbor? Another Christian View*. New York: Harper San Francisco, 1980.

Scroggs, Robin. *The New Testament and Homosexuality*. Minneapolis: Augsburg Fortress Press, 1984.

Sommer, Volker, and Paul L. Vasey. *Homosexual Behaviour in Animals: An Evolutionary Perspective*. Cambridge, England: Cambridge University Press, 2006.

Tolbert, Mary A. "Statement for Committee on Investigation," Presented at a hearing held by The United Methodist Church Northern California-Nevada Annual Conference Committee on Investigation for Clergy Members, Sacramento, California, February, 2000.

--------- "The Bible and Same-Gender Marriage," Presented at Wisconsin's for Marriage Equality Conference, December 4, 2004. Center for Lesbian and Gay Studies of the Pacific School of Religion, http://www.cafaithforequality.org/reflect.html (accessed March 21, 2009).

The Book of Discipline of the United Methodist Church 2008. Nashville, TN: The United Methodist Publishing House, 2008.

Vogel, Dwight W., "Homosexuality and the Church: Evangelical Commitment and Prophetic Responsibility," in *The Loyal Opposition: Struggling With the Church on Homosexuality*. Edited by Tex Sample and Amy E. DeLong. Nashville: Abingdon Press, 2000.

Weaver, Denny J. *The Nonviolent Atonement*. Grand Rapids, Michigan/Cambridge, U.K.: Eerdmans Publishing Company, 2001.

Werblowsky, Zwi, R. J., and Geoffrey Wigoder, Editors. *The Oxford Dictionary of The Jewish Religion*. Oxford/New York: The Oxford University Press, 1999.

Wesley, John. *John Wesley's Sermons: An Anthology*. Edited by Albert C. Outler and Richard P. Heitzenrater. Nashville, Tennessee: Abingdon Press, 1987.

Williams, Delores. *Sisters in the Wilderness: The Challenge of Womanist God-Talk*.Maryknoll, N.Y.: Orbis Books, 1993.

Wink, Walter, editor. *Homosexuality and Christian Faith. Questions of Conscience for the Churches*. Minneapolis: Augsburg Fortress Press, 1999.

Wink, Walter. *Jesus and Nonviolence: A Third Way*. Minneapolis: Fortress Press, 2003.

.........*The Powers That Be: Theology for a New Millennium*. New York: Random House, 1999.